'40s, '50s, & '60s Stemware by Tiffin

Schiffer Publishing Ltd®

4880 Lower Valley Road, Atglen, PA 19310 USA

Ed Goshe, Ruth Hemminger, & Leslie Piña

Book Design by Leslie Piña
Layout by Bonnie M. Hensley
Type set in ZapfChan Bd BT/GoudyOISt BT

ISBN: 0-7643-0869-6
Printed in China
1 2 3 4

Published by Schiffer Publishing Ltd.
4880 Lower Valley Road
Atglen, PA 19310
Phone: (610) 593-1777; Fax: (610) 593-2002
E-mail: Schifferbk@aol.com
Please visit our web site catalog at **www.schifferbooks.com**

In Europe, Schiffer books are distributed by Bushwood Books
6 Marksbury Avenue Kew Gardens
Surrey TW9 4JF England
Phone: 44 (0)181 392-8585; Fax: 44 (0)181 392-9876
E-mail: Bushwd@aol.com

This book may be purchased from the publisher.
Include $3.95 for shipping. Please try your bookstore first.
We are interested in hearing from authors with book ideas on related subjects.
You may write for a free printed catalog.

Contents

Acknowledgments

This volume documents many of the popular stemware patterns produced by the Tiffin Glass Company from 1940 to 1980. Due to the vast amount of patterns and stemlines produced, it is virtually impossible to include information on every line; some patterns remain undocumented. To make this volume as comprehensible as possible, we were aided by the following people with the loan of their glassware or information: Tracey and Aaron Sherman, King's Glass Engraving, Inc., Richard and Beverly Digby, G. and T. Boes, Ann Forrest, Martha Forrest, Carol J. Chaney, Dale and Eunice Cover, Richard and Virginia Distel, Dee and Tony Mondloch, Jon Eakin, Phil & Rayella Engle, Robert and Donna Overholt, Bill Reyer, Harold and Betty Scherger, Paul J. Williams, Martha Ziegler, Gene and Jodi Haugh, and Robert and Anne Jones.

We are grateful to those who assisted us at libraries and other public institutions, especially Carolyn Goshe and Bill Reyer for helping research the periodicals at the Carnegie Library of Pittsburgh, Pennsylvania; the Cleveland Public Library, Cleveland Ohio; and Rosalie Adams, Director of the Seneca County Museum for photographs, etchings, and other valuable information. Thanks also to John Bing for his assistance in preparing the manuscript, and Ramón Piña and Lyman Hemminger for the hours of assistance during the photo sessions.

Introduction

This book focuses on the stemware and tableware items that were produced from 1940 through 1980 at Factory R of the United States Glass Company located in Tiffin, Ohio. The bulk of the pressed tableware items were produced at Factory G of the United States Glass Company, located in Glassport, Pennsylvania; all blown ware was manufactured at Factory R. Beginning in 1927, products of Factory G and Factory R were marketed as Tiffinware.

Company terminology is used in the captions to describe items, with object and color names capitalized. The dimensions are measured at the widest point. An "h" indicates that the height is the largest dimension of the object.

A stemline number is determined by the combination of the shape of the bowl and the shape of the stem. The same stem, with a different shaped bowl would indicate a different stemline number. When describing two-tone objects, the predominant color is listed first, with the trim color following. The term "trim" refers to an additional color applied to the body of a glass object. For example, a Killarney goblet with Crystal trim indicates a Killarney bowl with an applied Crystal stem and foot.

Crystal was the predominate color of stemware and tableware produced from 1940 through 1980. Killarney, Wistaria, and Twilight, however, were also successfully produced on a variety of stemlines. A number of stemware blanks were marketed in the 1950s as Emerald, Emerald Green, Jade, and Shamrock; all these green colors were actually Tiffin's Killarney color. Azalea, Carnation, Cherry Blossom, and Wild Rose were all produced in a pale pink color on different stemware blanks in the mid 1950s, and are all the same color. Several old colors were renamed in the 1960s: Amethyst became Plum; Old Gold became Golden Banana; Amber became Desert Red; and Royal Blue became Cobalt Blue. Colored stemware produced in the late 1970s was often known by generic color names, e.g., Blue, Green, Amber, and Pink.

By 1940, the use of numerous optics in stemware had diminished. A Wide Optic was occasionally used; however, most blanks were produced plain, without an optic. A limited number of items were manufactured with Diamond Optic and Swedish optic.

A complete etching or engraving may not always appear on stemware. Large patterns were sometimes reduced in size to fit on a smaller bowl. An example is the elongated Melrose etching. Sometimes the lower portion of this pattern was necessarily removed.

Prices are listed in U.S. dollars at the end of the caption in **bold** type. Each item is priced using a value range. These values were derived from actual purchase prices, from prices seen at antique shows or shops, and an item's rarity and desirability. The prices are listed in the order in which the respective pieces appear in the photo. These values are intended as a guide, and *neither the authors nor the publisher are responsible for any transactions based on this guide.*

Glassmaking Terms

Acid Polishing – A process whereby a gray cutting is immersed in acid to achieve a polished finish.

Blank – An undecorated glass object.

Blown Glass – Glass objects produced by the forcing of air by a glassworker through a blowpipe into molten glass.

Bobeche – A circular piece of glass with a center hole used on a candlestick to catch melted wax.

Bubble Stem – An entrapment of air in a stem.

Compote (Comport) – A footed or stemmed bowl, usually used to hold candy, fruit, nuts, etc.

Crimped – The result of shaping the rim of a glass object into a scalloped edge.

Cruet – A handled and stoppered bottle, used to hold oil or vinegar.

Crystal – Clear or colorless glass.

Cutting – 1) A general term that describes the process of applying a design to a glass surface by the contact of the object against a rotating wheel. 2) The design or pattern that has been applied to a glass object.

Engraving – Another term for cutting a design on a glass object.

Filament Stem – A secondary color introduced inside a crystal stem.

Gray Cutting – An engraving that has not been hand or acid polished.

Inlay – The addition of gold, silver, or platinum over a plate etching.

Lead Glass – Glass to which lead has been added, to achieve brilliancy.

Line – A distinct line of glassware.

Nappy – A small dish, usually handled.

Plate Etching – A decoration applied to glassware by a process using a flat steel plate, ink, wax, and hydrofluoric acid.

Pressed Glass – Glassware that is formed by hand or machine made using a plunger to compress molten glass in a mold.

Sand Carving – A design applied to a glass object by means of a mini sand blaster, to achieve a gray cut appearance.

Satin Finish – A frosted appearance achieved by immersion in an acid bath.

Tableware – Items other than stemware with the same design or pattern.

Torte Plate – A large plate, 12 inches or larger, used to serve cake, cookies, etc.

History of the Tiffin Glass Company

Original United States Glass Company and Tiffin logos dating from the 1920s. These were supplied by the company to dealers or stores that sold Tiffin Glass. Original logos are extremely difficult to find today.

In July 1888, it was announced that the A. J. Beatty & Sons glass factory of Steubenville, Ohio, would be relocating to Tiffin, Ohio. A. J. Beatty had been negotiating with various communities for more than a year to establish a site for the new factory. The city of Tiffin offered five years of natural gas, $35,000 in cash, and land valued at $15,000. Construction of a three-furnace glass factory at the corner of Fourth Avenue and Vine Street began in September 1888, and operations commenced on August 15, 1889. Early production capacity was reported to be 500,000 pressed tumblers per week.

A. J. Beatty & Sons merged with the United States Glass Company on January 1, 1892, and became one of nineteen factories of the large corporation. The

Tiffin factory was designated Factory R. On May 23, 1893, less than two years later, Factory R was destroyed by fire. The factory was rebuilt in Tiffin in return for two additional years of free natural gas.

During the early years of the 1900s, there was a gradual shift from pressed to blown tableware, in response to customers' demands. A paper label identified the glass items with the letters USG intertwined within a gold-colored shield. Commercial ware continued to be marketed under the United States Glass Company name until September 1927. After that time, household goods were identified by a gold paper label with TIFFIN superimposed over a large "T" within a shield.

While other factories within the United States Glass Company were forced to close during the Great Depression of the 1930s, Factory R managed to survive. In June 1938, the offices of the United States Glass Company were transferred from Pittsburgh to Tiffin with C. W. Carlson as President. By 1940, all

Left: Typical gold colored Tiffin label which was applied to Tiffin Glass products from the 1920s through 1980.

Center: Blue colored Tiffin labels are far less often seen than gold colored labels. Blue labels are known on Tiffin Glass products dating from as early as the late 1930s, and used sparingly through the 1970s. A green colored label was also used, and these were used c.1979-1980.

Right: During the 1960s, a gold colored Tiffin label was used, which had the name of the stemware pattern on it.

September 1956 photograph of the United States Glass Company (Factory R) located in Tiffin, Ohio, at Fourth Avenue and Vine Street.

A. J. Beatty and Sons letterhead dated April 4, 1892, addressed to D. C. Ripley from R. J. Beatty.

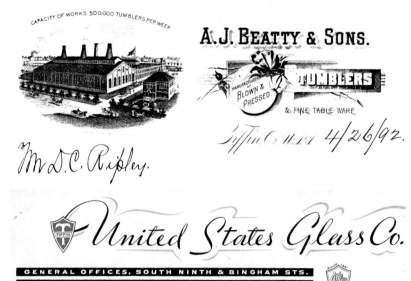

Bottom four pictures: United States Glass Company letterheads dating prior to 1938.

glassware was marked with a Tiffin label; however, the official name of the company remained the United States Glass Company through 1962.

In the 1940s, three major changes took place in the use of tableware by the American public, resulting in these transitions: Crystal stemware regained its popularity over colored stemware; fewer items were produced in each stemline; and to a large degree, china replaced the use of glass tableware for table settings.

Although the focus of Tiffin's production continued to be stemware, a new line of modern designs contributed to the prosperity of the Tiffin factory. In 1940, Mr. Carlson introduced the Swedish Modern line, consisting of heavy off-hand shapes. The Swedish Modern name was changed to Tiffin Modern in May 1946, to clarify that the glassware was American made. Interest in Tiffin Modern free-form designs continued into the 1960s.

The purchase of numerous Duncan and Miller Glass Company molds and equipment occurred in 1955. Several popular Duncan patterns were produced by the Tiffin and Glassport factories from 1956 until the closing of the Tiffin facility in 1980.

In 1958, serious financial difficulties arose within the corporation, resulting in the sale of the assets to a New York investment firm. Business conditions did not improve and a second sale took place in March 1961 to Brilhart Plastics Corporation of Mineola, New York. In 1962, bankruptcy occurred; however, the Tiffin factory remained open until early 1963.

Craftsmanship in Glass **Tiffin** ART GLASS CORPORATION

Tiffin, Ohio 44883
419-447-5313

1964 letterhead for the Tiffin Art Glass Corporation.

CONTINENTAL CAN COMPANY, INC.		INTERNAL CORRESPONDENCE	
T O	NAME: Paul J. Williams	**F R O M**	NAME: C. W. Carlson, Jr.
	LOCATION: Plant Engineer		LOCATION: DATE: 11/29/66

November 29, 1966, Continental Can Company inter-office memo.

Franciscan® crystal By **Tiffin**

INTERPACE CORPORATION
P. O. BOX 667
TIFFIN, OHIO 44883

1973 Franciscan Crystal letterhead.

Tiffin CRYSTAL
A DIVISION OF TOWLE SILVERSMITHS

Tiffin TOWLE

1982 Tiffin Crystal letterhead.

Charles W. Carlson, Sr. (1901-1979). C. W. Carlson's glassmaking career began in 1937 when he was chosen by the United States Reconstruction Finance Corporation to resolve the deep financial problems facing the United States Glass Company. Prior to this, he had been employed by a title company. According to his grandson, Michael Carlson, C. W. Carlson was not a lawyer as previously reported. A high school graduate with no additional formal education and no glass experience, Carlson was nevertheless an astute businessman with an eye for design that would dramatically change the course of the production of the United States Glass Company. Later his son, C.W. (Bill) Carlson, Jr., also played an important role in the history of the Tiffin Glass Company.

Cordon Blue.

Royal Medallion.

American Manor.

Reynolds Crystal.

Eternal Fine Crystal of
Covina, California. The fine
print reads "By Tiffin,
U.S.A."

The Renata Collection, Handmade
Crystal, Rickes-Crisa, Omaha,
Nebraska.

In that year, four former employees—Paul Williams, C. W. Carlson Jr., Ellsworth Beebe, and Bea Platt—bought the plant and renamed it the Tiffin Art Glass Company. Incorporation took place May 1, 1963. The start-up date for the new Tiffin venture was September 16, 1963. This transaction marked the end of the United States Glass Company. A great loss was incurred on August 3, 1963, when the Glassport factory was destroyed by a tornado. Nevertheless, business improved with $2,000,000 in annual sales.

On June 4, 1966, the company was sold again, this time to a major corporation, the Continental Can Company, in exchange for 6,462 shares of Continental common stock. The company was renamed the Tiffin Glass Company, Inc. During these years, stemware remained the major focus of production, with blown and pressed ware also manufactured.

The factory changed hands again when it was purchased in December 1968 by another large corporation, Interpace, the parent company of Franciscan, Shenango, and Mayer China companies. It continued to be known as the Tiffin Glass Company; but, in addition to using the gold Tiffin shield sticker, Interpace began to use a paper label, "Franciscan Crystal," which they placed on selected stemware lines in May 1969. This practice continued for two years. Interpace introduced several new stemware lines to coordinate with their china dinnerware patterns: Jubilation, Canterbury II, Flambeau, Revelation, Madeira, and Cabaret.

The Tiffin factory furnished a variety of stemware patterns to numerous companies for private distribution. As early as 1930, Tiffin was providing tableware to the Sears and Roebuck, and Montgomery-Ward companies, and they continued to provide stemware to various retail outlets through the 1970s. Among these companies were Tiffany's, Macy's, Colony House, Royal Medallion, Nancy

Prentiss, American Manor, and Reynolds Crystal. American Manor and Reynolds Crystal were subsidiaries of Interpace Corp., parent company of Tiffin Glass, 1969-1979. During this ten-year period, stemware in several new colors was introduced to coordinate with Interpace's Shenango China.

On May 10, 1979, the factory was sold for the last time to Towle Silversmiths and operated as Tiffin Crystal, a division of Towle Silversmiths. The furnaces were shut down on May 1, 1980, the date considered by collectors to be the end of the Tiffin Glass Company. The Outlet Store and a decorating shop remained open until October 1984, when the facility permanently closed. Towle later donated the factory and land to the city of Tiffin in exchange for a $1.1 million tax write-off. The city offered the property free to any company that would bring 100 jobs into the city. Unable to find a tenant, the city demolished part of the factory in late December 1985, and January 1986. Towle continued to sell Tiffin Glass stemware via mail order, including the popular pattern Palais Versailles, through at least 1990.

After production had ceased in 1980, the molds were dispersed and Russell Vogelsong of Summit Art Glass Company of Ravenna, Ohio, acquired the Tiffin shield trademark mold. The Tiffin Glass Collectors Club subsequently purchased this mold in 1991. To date, the logo has been reproduced in four colors: pink, cobalt blue, red, and green, some with satin or iridized finishes.

Over the years, Tiffin Glass products were identified by means of various paper labels. In 1969, a stylized Tiffin acid stamp was used to identify some stemware lines; this mark was used intermittently through the 1970s. Also during the 1970s, some products were marked by the application of an acid stamp of the Tiffin shield trademark.

Chapter 1
Plate Etchings

Three popular etchings were introduced in the 1940s: Cherokee Rose, June Night, and Rambling Rose. By 1950, the popularity of plate etchings on stemware had been largely replaced by engraved stemware. The number of stemware sizes also had been reduced.

Several new patterns were introduced in the 1950s and 1970s with limited success. Etchings were almost exclusively applied to Crystal blanks. A number of patterns was embellished with gold or platinum trim and inlay. Today, plate etchings have regained favor with collectors of fine stemware.

United States Glass Company 1942 pamphlet featuring the Connoisseur's Choice line by Tiffin Glass.

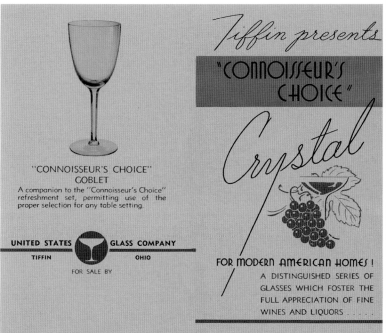

"CONNOISSEUR'S CHOICE" GOBLET

A companion to the "Connoisseur's Choice" refreshment set, permitting use of the proper selection for any table setting.

UNITED STATES GLASS COMPANY
TIFFIN   OHIO
FOR SALE BY

Tiffin presents
"CONNOISSEUR'S CHOICE"
Crystal
FOR MODERN AMERICAN HOMES!
A DISTINGUISHED SERIES OF GLASSES WHICH FOSTER THE FULL APPRECIATION OF FINE WINES AND LIQUORS . . . . .

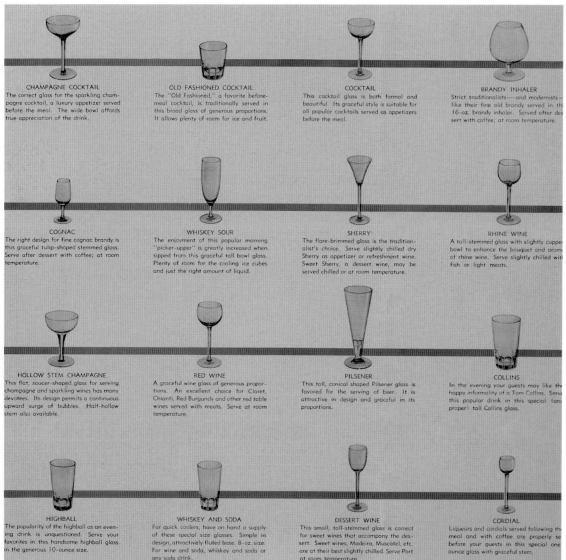

CHAMPAGNE COCKTAIL
The correct glass for the sparkling champagne cocktail, a luxury appetizer served before the meal. The wide bowl affords true appreciation of the drink.

OLD FASHIONED COCKTAIL
The "Old Fashioned," a favorite before-meal cocktail, is traditionally served in this broad glass of generous proportions. It allows plenty of room for ice and fruit.

COCKTAIL
This cocktail glass is both formal and beautiful. Its graceful style is suitable for all popular cocktails served as appetizers before the meal.

BRANDY INHALER
Strict traditionalists — and modernists — like their fine old brandy served in this 16-oz. brandy inhaler. Served after dessert with coffee; at room temperature.

COGNAC
The right design for fine cognac brandy is this graceful tulip-shaped stemmed glass. Serve after dessert with coffee; at room temperature.

WHISKEY SOUR
The enjoyment of this popular morning "picker-upper" is greatly increased when sipped from this graceful tall bowl glass. Plenty of room for the cooling ice cubes and just the right amount of liquid.

SHERRY
The flare-brimmed glass is the traditionalist's choice. Serve slightly chilled dry Sherry as appetizer or refreshment wine. Sweet Sherry, a dessert wine, may be served chilled or at room temperature.

RHINE WINE
A tall-stemmed glass with slightly cupped bowl to enhance the bouquet and aroma of rhine wine. Serve slightly chilled with fish or light meats.

HOLLOW STEM CHAMPAGNE
This flat, saucer-shaped glass for serving champagne and sparkling wines has many devotees. Its design permits a continuous upward surge of bubbles. Half-hollow stem also available.

RED WINE
A graceful wine glass of generous proportions. An excellent choice for Claret, Chianti, Red Burgundy and other red table wines served with meats. Serve at room temperature.

PILSENER
This tall, conical shaped Pilsener glass is favored for the serving of beer. It is attractive in design and graceful in its proportions.

COLLINS
In the evening your guests may like the happy informality of a Tom Collins. Serve this popular drink in this special (and proper) tall Collins glass.

HIGHBALL
The popularity of the highball as an evening drink is unquestioned. Serve your favorites in this handsome highball glass in the generous 10-ounce size.

WHISKEY AND SODA
For quick coolers, have on hand a supply of these special size glasses. Simple in design, attractively fluted base. 8-oz. size. For wine and soda, whiskey and soda or any soda drink.

DESSERT WINE
This small, tall-stemmed glass is correct for sweet wines that accompany the dessert. Sweet wines, Madeira, Muscatel, etc. are at their best slightly chilled. Serve Port at room temperature.

CORDIAL
Liqueurs and cordials served following the meal and with coffee are properly served before your guests in this special one-ounce glass with graceful stem.

Top left: Alexandria
The Alexandria etching was introduced in 1979 as part of the Tiffin Tradition line. This same poppy motif etching was used for the Flanders pattern in the 1920s and for the St. Gallen etching with platinum inlay in 1979.
#17725, Rambler Rose gold band and inlay: Goblet. **$85-110**.

Bottom left: Detail of Alexandria etching.

Top right: Alexandria
#17725 Rambler Rose gold band and inlay: Goblet, **$85-110**; Sherry, **$85-110**; #1 Wine, **$85-110**; Cordial, **$100-125**.

Bottom right: Antoinette
The Antoinette etching was introduced in 1979 on the #17594 stemline. This etching originally appeared in the 1940s as Bouquet on the #17301 stemline.
Crystal #17594, bubble stem, Laurel gold band: Goblet, **$75-100**; Wine, **$75-100**; Champagne/Sherbet, **$65-95**; Ice Tea, **$75-100**.

Opposite page:
Top left: Bouquet
The Bouquet etching was used in the 1940s on stemline #17301. This same etching appeared on two Killarney stemlines in the late 1940s and was called Bouquette Green. This etching reappeared as Antoinette on stemline #17594 in 1979. Crystal #17301: Goblet; Cordial; Apollo gold band. **$30-40**; **$45-55**.

Bottom left: Detail of Bouquet etching.

Right: Bouquet, 8" h. Vase, Apollo gold band, undocumented line number. **$75-100**.

12

Bouquette Green
Killarney with Crystal trim #17394: Champagne, **$55-75**; Ice Tea, **$65-85**; Wine, **$55-75**; Goblet, **$65-85**; Cocktail, **$55-75**.

Top: Bouquette Green
The Bouquette Green etching was produced in the late 1940s. This same etching was used earlier on the #17301 stemline in Crystal and was known as Bouquet. A 1979 offering with a Laurel gold band was called Antoinette. Killarney with Crystal trim, #17394, Apollo gold band, gold inlay, Goblet. **$65-85**.

Bottom: Detail of Bouquette Green etching.

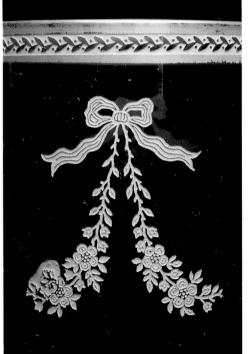

Bouquette Green
Killarney with Crystal trim #15074 Cocktails. **$65-85** each.

Bouquette Green
Killarney with Crystal trim #17430: 6" h. Rose Bowl, **$200-250**; 10 ¼" h. Urn Vase, **$200-250**; 6" h. Sweet Pea Vase, **$175-225**; all with gold inlay and Apollo gold band.

Cherokee Rose

This rose motif etching was produced on the #17399 and #17403 stemlines. Introduced circa 1941, Cherokee Rose remains popular with collectors today. During the 1940s, Cherokee Rose was a "protected" pattern; retail stores carrying Cherokee Rose retained exclusive selling rights to this pattern within a 125 mile radius in some areas. Goblet, **$20-30**.

United States Glass Company

1941 United States Glass Company catalog page featuring the Cherokee Rose etching.

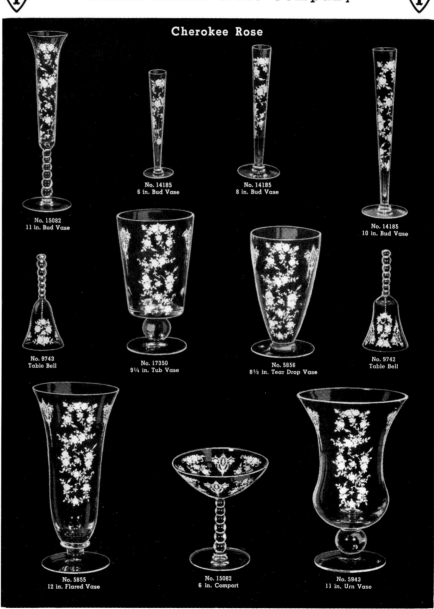

Cherokee Rose

No. 15082
11 in. Bud Vase

No. 14185
6 in. Bud Vase

No. 14185
8 in. Bud Vase

No. 14185
10 in. Bud Vase

No. 9743
Table Bell

No. 17350
9¼ in. Tub Vase

No. 5856
8½ in. Tear Drop Vase

No. 9742
Table Bell

No. 5855
12 in. Flared Vase

No. 15082
6 in. Comport

No. 5943
11 in. Urn Vase

Tiffin, Ohio

Detail of Cherokee Rose etching.

16

Cherokee Rose

No. 17399
9 oz. Goblet

No. 17399
3½ oz. Wine

No. 17399
4 oz. Claret

No. 17399
5½ oz. Saucer Champ.

No. 17399
3½ oz. Cocktail

No. 17399
1 oz. Cordial

No. 17399
5½ oz. Sundae

No. 17399
5 oz. Ftd. Tumbler

No. 17399
8 oz. Ftd. Tumbler

No. 17399
4½ oz. Parfait

No. 14196
4½ oz. Oyster Cocktail

No. 17399
2 oz. Sherry

No. 14196
12 oz. Finger Bowl

No. 17399
10½ oz. Ice Tea

Cherokee Rose

No. 5902
Sugar

No. 5902
Cream

No. 5859
Pitcher

No. 5902
10 in. Salad Bowl

No. 5902
3 Pc. Mayonnaise Set

No. 5902
Candlestick

No. 5902
13 in. Cone Centerpiece

No. 5902
12½ in. Flared Centerpiece

No. 5902
12 in. Crimped Centerpiece

Tiffin, Ohio

Tiffin, Ohio

Cherokee Rose.

Cherokee Rose.

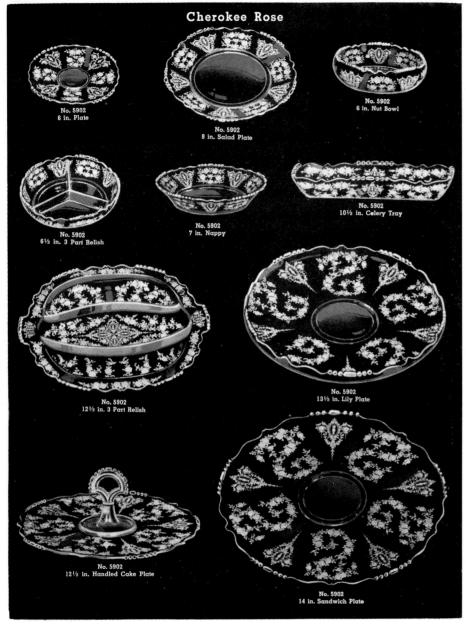

Cherokee Rose

No. 5902
6 in. Plate

No. 5902
8 in. Salad Plate

No. 5902
6 in. Nut Bowl

No. 5902
6½ in. 3 Part Relish

No. 5902
7 in. Nappy

No. 5902
10½ in. Celery Tray

No. 5902
12½ in. 3 Part Relish

No. 5902
13½ in. Lily Plate

No. 5902
12½ in. Handled Cake Plate

No. 5902
14 in. Sandwich Plate

Tiffin, Ohio

Cherokee Rose.

Cherokee Rose
Crystal #5902: 12 ½" 3-part Relish, **$50-75**; Cream and Sugar, **$40-$50** set; 10 ½" Celery Tray, **$35-45**.

Cherokee Rose
Crystal #5902: 8" Salad Plate, **$15-20**; 14" Sandwich Plate, **$50-75**; #2, 3" h. Salt and Pepper, **$150-175** pair; 6" Plate, **$10-15**.

Cherokee Rose
Crystal #17399: 1 oz. Cordial, **$40-50**; 9 oz. Goblet, **$25-35**; 3 ½ oz. Wine, **$25-35**; 10 ½ oz. Ice Tea, **$20-30**; 5 ½ oz. Sundae, **$15-25**; 5 ½ oz. Saucer Champagne, **$15-25**; 8 oz. Footed Tumbler, **$15-25**.

Top left: Cherokee Rose
Crystal #5902: 12 ½" Flared Centerpiece
Bowl, **$65-90**; 7 ¾" Candlestick, **$40-$50**.

Bottom left: Cherokee Rose
Crystal #14185, 10" h. Bud Vase, Platinum
trim, **$45-65**; #14185, 8" h. Bud Vase,
$20-40; #14185, 6" h. Bud Vase, **$15-35**;
#15082, 11 ½" h. Bud Vase, **$55-75**.

Top center: Cherokee Rose
Crystal: #9742 Table Bell; #9743 Table
Bell; #2 Salt and Pepper. **$40-60**; **$40-60**;
$150-175 pair.

Bottom center: Cherokee Rose
Crystal: #14196, 4 ½ oz. Oyster Cocktail;
#17403, 4 ½ oz. Parfait; #17403, 1 oz.
Cordial. **$25-35**; **$50-60**; **$40-$50**.

Top right: Cherokee Rose
Crystal #5909-8, 12" Center Handled Cake
Plate, Pearl Edge Line, 1948. **$175-200**.

Top left: Cherokee Rose
Crystal #14194, 2 qt. Jug. **$500-
600**.

Top center: Cherokee Rose
Crystal: #5909-9, 12 ½", two
handled Cake Plate; #5909-10, 8"
Oblong Bread Tray, Pearl Edge line,
1948. **$55-75** each.

Top right: Cherokee Rose
Crystal: #5902, 10" Salad Bowl;
#5902, 12" Crimped Centerpiece.
$90-115 each.

Bottom left: Cherokee Rose
Crystal with Gold Inlay #5855, 12"
h. Flared vase. **$400-500**.

Bottom right: Side view of #5855
Vase.

Top left: Cherokee Rose
Crystal #5902, 7 ½" Candlesticks with Bobeches and Prisms, **$150-175** pair.

Top right: Twilight #17690 Goblets with June Night, Fuchsia, and Cherokee Rose etchings. **$50-75** each. These goblets were non-production items, produced in the late 1970s.

Bottom row, left to right:
Detail of June Night etching.
Detail of Fuchsia etching.
Detail of Cherokee Rose etching.
January 1950 advertisement by the United States Glass Company appearing in *Crockery and Glass Journal* featuring Cherokee Rose.

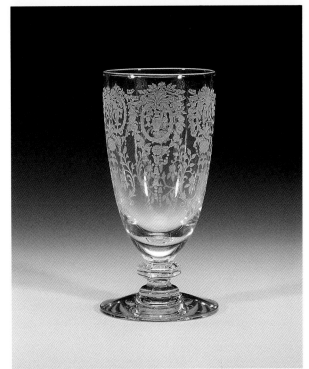

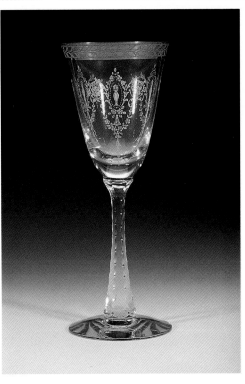

Top left: Talisman
Produced in the early 1940s on stemlines #17399 and #17403, this pattern is identical to the Cherokee Rose etching. Talisman is decorated with a gold band. Crystal #17399, 5 ½ oz. Champagne, gold band. **$20-30**.

Top center: Queen Anne
Produced circa 1940s, the Queen Anne etching has an urn motif similar to the Cherokee Rose pattern. Crystal #17453 Footed Tumbler. **$10-15**.

Top right: Detail of Queen Anne etching.

Bottom left: Gold Medallion #17724
Included in the Tiffin Tradition line, Gold Medallion featured the cameo etching of the 1940s Cherokee Rose pattern. #17724: #2 Wine, Flute Champagne, Sherry, all with cut stem, gold inlay, and Laurel gold band. **$75-100** each.

Bottom center: Gold Medallion
Crystal #17724 Sherry, cut stem, gold inlay, Laurel gold band. **$75-100**.

Bottom right: Detail of Gold Medallion etching.

23

Enchantment
#17507, platinum trim, Goblet, Wine, Champagne/Sherbet, Ice Tea. **$15-25** each.

Enchantment
Detail of etching.

1980 advertisement featuring the Enchantment etching.

Top left: Damask Rose #17477. **$20-30**.

Bottom left: Enchantment
The Enchantment etching was used in 1980 on the #17507 stemline. This etching was previously used on stemline #17701 circa 1971, and was known as Moon Glow. Crystal #17507, platinum trim, Goblet. **$15-25**.

Imperial Forest
Crystal #17725: #2 Wine, Goblet, Flute
Champagne, all with platinum inlay and
Minton platinum band. **$75-100** each.

Imperial Forest
Imperial Forest was introduced in 1979
as part of the Tiffin Tradition line. This
etching was decorated with platinum
inlay only. Crystal #17725 Goblet,
platinum inlay and Minton platinum
band. **$75-100**.

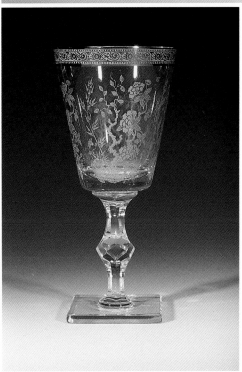

Bottom right: Detail of Imperial
Forest etching.

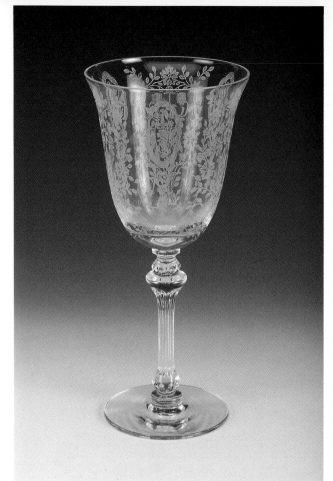

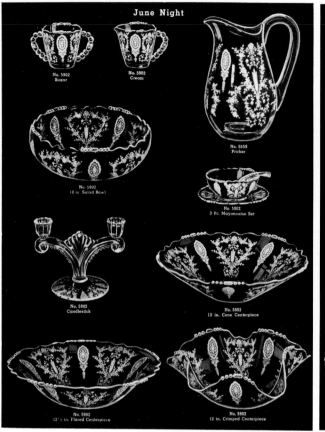

June Night

No. 5902
Sugar

No. 5902
Cream

No. 5859
Pitcher

No. 5902
10 in. Salad Bowl

No. 5902
3 Pc. Mayonnaise Set

No. 5902
Candlestick

No. 5902
13 in. Cone Centerpiece

No. 5902
12½ in. Flared Centerpiece

No. 5902
12 in. Crimped Centerpiece

Tiffin, Ohio

June Night

No. 5902
6 in. Plate

No. 5902
8 in. Salad Plate

No. 5902
6 in. Nut Bowl

No. 5902
6½ in. 3 Part Relish

No. 5902
7 in. Nappy

No. 5902
10½ in. Celery Tray

No. 5902
12½ in. 3 Part Relish

No. 5902
13½ in. Lily Plate

No. 5902
12½ in. Handled Cake Plate

No. 5902
14 in. Sandwich Plate

Tiffin, Ohio

Top left: June Night
This popular etching was designed by J.F. Downing in 1941, and was produced on several stemlines, with the #17378 and the #17392 stemlines being the most commonly found. The Love Lace pattern, which is identical to the June Night etching, was produced on stemline #17358. The Cherry Laurel etching, which is found on stemline #17392, also is identical to the June Night etching; however, a gold band was added to the stemware and tableware. #17392 Goblet. $20-30.

Bottom left: Detail of June Night etching.

Top center: 1941 United States Glass Company catalog page featuring the June Night etching.

Top right: June Night.

26

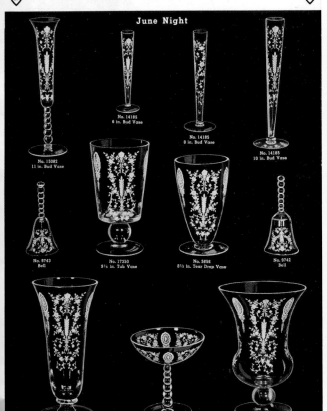

June Night

No. 15082
11 in. Bud Vase

No. 14185
6 in. Bud Vase

No. 14185
8 in. Bud Vase

No. 14185
10 in. Bud Vase

No. 9743
Bell

No. 17350
9¼ in. Tub Vase

No. 5856
8½ in. Tear Drop Vase

No. 9742
Bell

No. 5855
12 in. Flared Vase

No. 15082
6 in. Comport

No. 5943
11 in. Urn Vase

Tiffin, Ohio

June Night

No. 17392
10 oz. Goblet

No. 17392
3 oz. Wine

No. 17392
4½ oz. Claret

No. 17392
6½ oz. Saucer Champ.

No. 17392
3½ oz. Cocktail

No. 17392
1¼ oz. Cordial

No. 17392
6½ oz. Sundae

No. 17392
5 oz. Ftd. Tumbler

No. 17392
9 oz. Ftd. Tumbler

No. 17392
5½ oz. Parfait

No. 14196
4½ oz. Oyster Cocktail

No. 17392
2½ oz. Sherry

No. 14196
12 oz. Finger Bowl

No. 17392
12 oz. Ice Tea

Tiffin, Ohio

Top left: June Night.

Top center: June Night.

Top right: June Night
Crystal #17392, 1 oz. Cordial; #14194, 2 qt. Jug with cover. **$40-$50; $550-650.**

Bottom right: June Night
Crystal #5902 Sugar and Cream; #15082, 6" Comport. **$40-$50** set; **$90-115.**

June Night
Crystal #17392: 6 ½ oz. Saucer Champagne, **$15-25**; 3 ½ oz. Cocktail, **$15-25**; 9 oz. Footed Tumbler, **$20-30**; 1 ¼ oz. Cordial, **$40-$50**; 5 oz. Footed Tumbler, **$15-25**; #5902, 7 ½" Candlestick, **$40-$50**.

Top right: October 1941 *China, Glass and Lamps* advertisement of the June Night etching by the United States Glass Company.

Bottom right: June 1942 *China and Glass* advertisement of the June Night etching by the United States Glass Company.

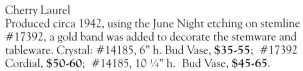

Cherry Laurel
Produced circa 1942, using the June Night etching on stemline #17392, a gold band was added to decorate the stemware and tableware. Crystal: #14185, 6" h. Bud Vase, **$35-55**; #17392 Cordial, **$50-60**; #14185, 10 ¼" h. Bud Vase, **$45-65**.

Love Lace
The Love Lace etching is identical to the June Night pattern. It was produced circa 1942 on stemline #17358. Crystal #17358 Goblet. **$25-35**.

Top right: Lord's Prayer
Killarney #5962, 8" Plate with etched Lord's Pray (Protestant Version) with gold inlay. Two versions, Catholic and Protestant, of the Lord's Prayer were etched on the 8" plates, c. 1948. **$50-70**.

Bottom right: Lord's Prayer
Crystal #5831, 7 ½" Plate, etched Lord's Prayer (Protestant Version) with gold inlay. A 4" tumbler was also etched with the Lord's Prayer. **$35-55**.

Melrose Green
The Melrose etching was used extensively from the 1920s through the 1970s on several stemlines. When applied to Killarney blanks, the etching was known as Melrose Green. The latter was produced in the late 1940s. Killarney with Crystal trim, #15074, gold inlay, Melrose gold band. **$75-100.**

Melrose Green
Killarney with Crystal trim #17394 Goblet with gold inlay and Melrose gold band. **$65-90.**

Top left: Magnolia #17477. **$20-30.**

Bottom left: Magnolia #17546. **$20-30.**

Opposite page:
Melrose Green
Killarney with Crystal trim #15074: Ice Tea, **$65-90**; Cocktail, **$65-90**; Wine, **$75-100**; Goblet, **$75-100**; Champagne, **$65-90**; all with gold inlay and Melrose gold band.

Melrose Green
Killarney with Crystal trim #17394: Juice, $50-75; Wine,
$55-80; Ice Tea, $55-80; Goblet, $65-90; all with gold inlay
and Melrose gold band.

Melrose Green
Killarney with Crystal trim #17430, 6" h. Sweet Pea Vase, **$175-225**; #6037, 5" Candlestick, **$75-100**; #17430, 10 ¼" h. Daisy Vase, **$200-250**; #17430, 6 ¼" Compote, **$100-125**; all with gold inlay and Melrose gold band.

Melrose Green
Killarney with Crystal trim #17430, 6 ¼" Large Rose bowl, with gold inlay and Melrose gold band. **$250-300**.

Melrose Green
Killarney with Crystal trim #17430, 9 ¼" Teardrop Vase, with gold inlay and Melrose gold band. **$250-300**.

Melrose #17358, Melrose gold band, Cordial, Wine, Goblet, Champagne/Sherbet, Cocktail. **$75-100; $60-85; $60-85; $55-80; $55-80.**

Top row: Killarney #17394; Melrose Green #17394, Melrose gold band; Bouquette Green #17394, Apollo gold band. **$20-30; $65-90; $65-90.**
Bottom row: Cherokee Rose #17403; Saturn #17403, gold band; #17390 stemline. **$25-35; $15-25; $15-25.**

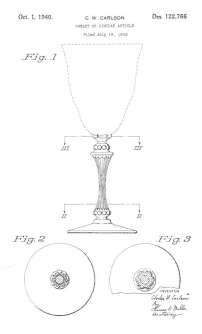

Oct. 1, 1940.   C. W. CARLSON   Des. 122,766
GOBLET OR SIMILAR ARTICLE
Filed July 19, 1940

Fig. 1

Fig. 2   *Fig. 3*

INVENTOR
Charles W. Carlson
By
Thomas E. Miller
his attorney

July 19, 1940, patent record for the #17358 stemline, designed by Charles W. Carlson.

May 13, 1941.   C. W. CARLSON   Des. 127,154

GOBLET OR SIMILAR ARTICLE

Filed March 4, 1941

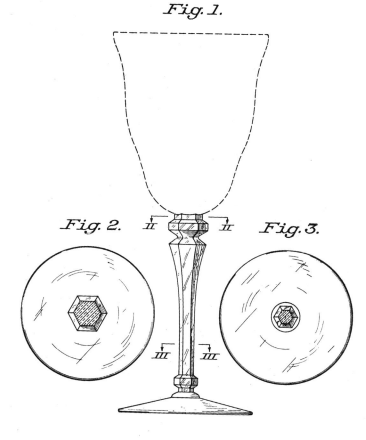

Fig. 1.

Fig. 2.   *Fig. 3.*

INVENTOR

Charles W. Carlson
by Thomas G. Miller
his attorney

Top left: Melrose #17356, Melrose gold band, Goblet, Wine, Champagne/Sherbet, Ice Tea. $60-85; $60-85; $55-80; $60-85.

Bottom left: The Melrose etching in the process of being transferred to a tumbler.

Right: March 4, 1941, patent for the #17356 stemline, designed by Charles W. Carlson.

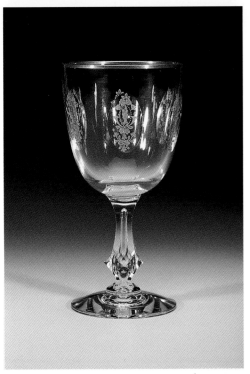

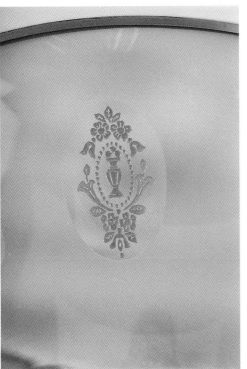

Top left: Palais Versailles #17594

The Palais Versailles pattern, which was introduced in 1954, features the Cameo etching with 24 k. gold inlay on the ground punty. This pattern was selected by the United States Glass Company to represent the fine quality of stemware produced at the Tiffin factory. Palais Versailles was used extensively in the company's advertising campaigns. This popular pattern was produced continuously from its introduction through 1980, and it remains a favorite with aficionados of fine crystal. Palais Versailles was produced on stemline #17594; Chateau Remond, which features the same gold encrusted Cameo etching, was produced on stemline #17591. Crystal #17594 Goblet, gold inlay, bubble stem. **$75-100**.

Bottom left: Detail of Palais Versailles etching.

Palais Versailles
Crystal #17594, Claret, **$70-95**; #1 Seafood Cocktail with liner, **$75-100**; #17594 Goblet, **$75-100**; Wine, **$70-95**; Ice Tea, **$70-95**; Juice, **$65-90**; Champagne/Sherbet, **$65-90**; Cordial, **$125-150**; Flute Champagne, **$85-110**; #453, 14 oz. Double Old Fashion, **$65-90**; #517, 12 oz. Hi Ball, **$65-90**.

37

Palais Versailles
Crystal: #1070, 4 ½" Fingerbowl, **$50-75**; #8833, 8" Salad Plate, **$50-75**; #8835, 10 ½" Dinner Plate, **$100-125**; #5501, 6 ¼" Compote, **$150-175**; #8834, 8" Crescent Salad Plate, **$50-75**.

Top right: Marie Bour painting the gold rim of a Palais Versailles goblet.

Bottom right: Tiffin Glass Company placard promoting Palais Versailles stemware.

CRYSTAL BY TIFFIN

Tiffin's gold-accented Palais Versailles stem strikes the regal keynote for this opulent setting.* See Palais Versailles at fine shops everywhere. Write TABLETOP™ 550 Fifth Avenue, New York, NY 10036 for your nearest retailer.

*Sterling: Edward VII from Frank Smith
China: Royal Tettau's Marquise from H. Wittur
Placemat: Contessa

As seen in House Beautiful and House and Garden

Palais Versailles
Crystal: #17594 Wine, $70-95; #5501, 6 ¼" Compote,
$150-175; #17594 Cordial, $125-150; Ice Tea, $70-95;
Champagne/Sherbet, $65-90; #8834, 8" Crescent Salad
Plate, $50-75; #8833, 8" Plate, $50-75; #17594 Goblet,
$75-100. All with gold trim.

39

Killarney with Crystal trim #17637 Cocktail, **$65-90**; #17637 Cordial, **$75-100**; #8833, 8" Salad Plate, **$50-75**; all with gold inlay. Produced circa 1954 for a limited period of time with the same gold encrusted etching as Palais Versailles.

Cameo
The Cameo design was taken from the "cameo" portion of the Cherokee Rose etching, circa 1954. Gold inlay was added to the Cameo etching to create the Palais Versailles pattern. Miss Margaret Truman chose the Cameo pattern for her wedding crystal in 1956. Crystal #17594: Goblet, **$20-30**; Cordial, **$30-40**; Champagne/Sherbet, **$15-25**; Wine, **$20-30**, Bubble stem.

Detail of Cameo etching.

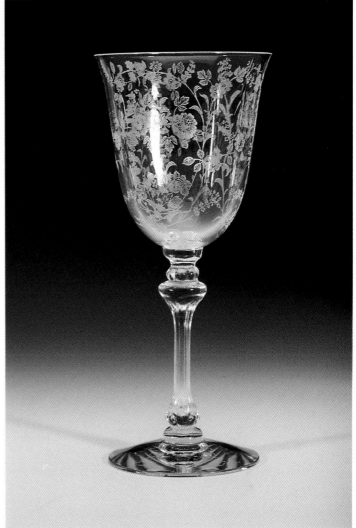

Chateau Remond
Introduced circa 1954, the Chateau Remond etching is identical to the Palais Versailles pattern, but appears on the #17591 stemline. Crystal #17591 Goblet, **$45-55**; Cordial, **$55-65**; Wine, **$45-55**; with gold inlay.

Top right: Rambling Rose
Rambling Rose, designed by J.F. Downing and introduced in 1948, was one of several plate etched Rose motif patterns by the United States Glass Company. Rambling Rose was produced on stemline #17392 only; this same etching with gold inlay on stemline #17392 was named Evening Rose. When the Rambling Rose etching is found on stemline #17378, it is known as Tiffin Rose. Crystal #17392 Goblet. **$20-30**.

Bottom left: Detail of Rambling Rose etching.

Bottom right: Rambling Rose
#17392: Goblet, Wine, Champagne/Sherbet, Ice Tea. **$20-30** each.

Tiffin Rose
The Tiffin Rose pattern, which is identical to the Rambling Rose pattern, was produced on stemline #17378 and #17441, beginning in 1948. Crystal: #17441 Goblet, **$20-30**; #17441 Cordial, **$30-40**; #5909-26, 8" Salad Plate (Pearl Edge line), **$10-15**; #17441 Champagne, **$15-25**.

Top right: Tiffin Rose Crystal #17441 Goblet. **$20-30**.

Bottom right: Detail of Tiffin Rose etching.

Top left: October 1948 *Crockery and Glass Journal* advertisement for the Tiffin Rose etching by the United States Glass Company.

Top center: Rose
Stemware with the Rose etching was made in crystal, circa mid 1950s, on stemlines #17453, #17474, and #17477. This etching was also produced on stemline #17477 in Wistaria. Crystal #17474 Goblet. **$15-25.**

Top right: Rose #17477. **$20-30.**

Bottom left: Rose
Wistaria with Crystal trim #17477 Goblet, Champagne, Wine. **$45-55** each.

Bottom right: Detail of Rose etching.

Top left: Damask Rose
Damask Rose was produced circa mid 1950s on stemlines #17474 in Crystal and #17477 in Crystal and Wistaria. There was limited production of this etching on stemline #17724 in the late 1970s. Crystal #17724 Goblet, gold inlay. **$35-45.**

Top center: Black, #17701 Goblet, platinum band; #17701 Goblet, gold encrusted, Tea Rose etching, very limited production, late 1970s. **$15-25**; **$20-30**.

Top right: Detail of Tea Rose etching.

Bottom left: Rose of Picardy
#17507. **$20-30.**

Bottom right: Tea Rose
#17453. **$20-30.**

Shah

The Shah etching was produced on stemline #17594 in the mid 1970s. The etching consists of a palm tree over crossed swords within a ground punty. This pattern was ordered by Boeing Aircraft especially for the Shah of Iran in 1977. Tiffin charged $270 for each stem and reportedly lost money on them, because of the precision required to make the ground punty. Crystal: #17594 Ice Tea, **$25-35**; #17594 Goblet, **$30-40**; #517, 14 oz. Hi Ball, **$25-35**; #517 Juice, **$25-35**, bubble stem; all with platinum trim.

Detail of Shah cutting.

Top left: Springtime #17434. **$20-30.**

Bottom left: Sunnyvale #17477, platinum trim. **$25-35.**

Top center: Springtime #17453. **$20-30.**

Bottom center: Detail of Victorian etching.

Victorian
Produced in 1979 as one of the Tiffin Tradition patterns. The Victorian etching borrows the cameo design from the popular Classic etching of the 1920s. Crystal #17724: #1 Wine, **$30-40**; Goblet, **$30-40**; Cordial **$50-60**, Laurel band.

Top left: Whisper
The Whisper etching was produced in the late 1970s with or without gold inlay. Crystal #17726: Ice Tea and Goblet, bubble stem, gold band. **$20-30** each.

Bottom left: Whisper #17726 bubble stem, gold trim: Goblet, Wine, Champagne/Sherbet, Ice Tea. **$20-30** each.

Top right: Whisper
Crystal #17657 Goblet, with gold inlay. **$25-35**.

Bottom right: Detail of Whisper etching.

Top left photo:
Top left: Moonglow #17701, platinum trim. **$15-25**.
Top right: Renaissance #17701, gold or platinum trim. **$15-25**.
Bottom left: Elyse #17683. **$15-25**.
Bottom right: Atwater #17701. **$15-25**.

Top center: Emil Walk attaching a stem to a champagne, c.late 1940s.

Top right: Archie Kahler blowing molten glass into a mold, c.late 1940s.

Bottom left: Early 1970s Franciscan Crystal Company photo promoting the Rambling Rose, Fuchsia, and Melrose etchings.

Chapter 2
Cuttings and Engravings

Cuttings and engravings played a major role in the production of Tiffin stemware from 1910 through 1980. Cuttings refer to geometric or mitre designs, e.g., Elyse; while engravings deviate from a straight, flat pattern to a more fluid, graceful design, e.g., Parkwood. Although the men and women cutters referred to these designs as engravings, company records reference the patterns as cuttings. Thousands of designs were produced with gray or polished cuttings. Numerous machine-cut patterns were also included in Tiffin's inventory.

TIFFIN STEMWARE

America's prestige crystal
. . . hand fashioned lead crystal
. . . designed by Tiffin for everyone!

Each of the stemware patterns shown in this section has seven basic stems: goblet, champagne-sherbet, claret, iced tea, juice, cocktail and cordial. In addition, we also furnish an 8" salad plate, finger-bowl, dessert nappy and seafood cocktail with liner. We are illustrating below the seven stems available in each of the thirteen different blank shapes which comprise Tiffin's active line.

| STYLE 17594 |
| STYLE 17640 |
| STYLE 17646 |
| STYLE 17651 |
| STYLE 17664 |
| STYLE 17665 |
| STYLE 17679 |
| STYLE 17680 |
| STYLE 17683 |
| STYLE 17684 |
| STYLE 17685 |
| STYLE 17687 |
| STYLE 17691 |

Renaissance
RHAPSODY

SHAPE 17352

Here is graceful, formal beauty—stately, rhapsodic beauty that breathes all the dazzling pomp and circumstance of a regal court in the Late Renaissance. The foot is simple and unadorned but the long, faceted stem strikes up a delicate note of beauty that flows into the radiant bowl and sprays out in long, arched lancets. Rhapsody offers a new and distinctive motif in fine stemware.

10-12-30-39   Printed in U. S. A.

SETTING THE STYLE IN STEMWARE FOR 1940

A Graceful Shape with Cut or Etched Bowl

EPERNAY
SHAPE 15001

Epernay speaks softly of early American days, whispers of expansive Colonial hospitality and lavish cordiality. Epernay, tall, graceful and shimmering with a pristine sparkle that rises from its graceful foot, gleams up through the elegantly knopped stem and bursts into full effulgence in the finely cut diamond and lancet design that embellishes the well proportioned bowl. A true aristocrat of the early American motif now in vogue.

JULIA
SHAPE 15001

The same beautiful symmetric shape of her lovely sister Epernay, but crowned with an exquisite, ornamental pattern delicately etched into the unconstrained beauty of the bowl. The finely etched design speaks of dignity and enchantment in perfect complement to the gleaming, unadorned beauty of foot and stem. Definitely caters to the vogue for early American service.

United States Glass Co.   -   Tiffin, Ohio

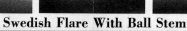

Swedish Flare With Ball Stem

GRIPSHOLM
SHAPE 17349

Only the ancient castle of good King Grip could challenge the rugged beauty of this new design and shape, called Gripsholm. Gripsholm rises swiftly from the simple, uncut beauty of the foot and ball stem and breaks with forceful, virile grace into strong, flare-shaped proportions of the handsome bowl.

In the beautiful, two-toned hand-cut design, slender stems reach up to support delicately-cut lancets that rest upon them.

KUNGSHOLM
SHAPE 17349

Kungsholm, strong and noble brother of Gripsholm, but even a bit more emphatic in the beautiful simplicity of the clean, refined design hand-cut on its bowl. Kungsholm has the same gleaming ball-stem, the same sweeping but simple lines of the flaring bowl—characteristic of this widely favored Swedish family. But in the finely-cut design of the Kungsholm, graceful, blade-like lancets leap from the sides by fives and spread out symmetrically into the shimmering crystal spray.

QUEEN ASTRID
SHAPE 17349

Queen Astrid—regal, resplendent, and beautiful—just like the lovely Swedish princess who became Queen. Queen Astrid embodies all the strong simplicity of her two stalwart brothers in shape, but on her glistening bowl she wears a delicately etched floral design that all but takes ones breath away by its dainty, lacy beauty. For refined, elegant etching in glassware, Queen Astrid transcends all ordinary beauty and grace.

This same delicate etching is also available in the new tall stem shape 17351 of Queen Astrid design.

English Short Stem with Cut Foot

TRAFALGAR
SHAPE 17348

Trafalgar—is definitely as English as its famous name. Its simple beauty is well-grounded for the clean, ornately-cut design of olives and ovals sparkle in a circular pattern about the graceful foot. After flowing through the symmetrically knopped stem, the pattern leaps up into the full, crystal clear sweep of the rounded bowl and stops only for the strong, horizontal band of diamond cutting which encircles the whole otherwise unadorned motif of the graceful bowl adding gem-like brilliance.

QUEEN ELIZABETH
SHAPE 17348

Queen Elizabeth, another cutting on this noble shape, so distinctly English in its pattern, displays in her design all the gay sparkle and resplendent pomp of the good Queen's lavish court. Clusters of graceful lancets flare out in the chaste and straight-forward design of the hand-cut foot. The simple but abundant diamond cutting dominates the design by almost completely covering the full, rounded bowl of glistening crystal.

Apollo #17670. $15-25.

April #17492, introduced 1951. $15-25.

Arabesque
Crystal Goblet and Champagne with cut
prism stem. $175-200 each.

Detail of cut prism stem.

Astral #17477, introduced 1951. **$15-25**.

Balfour #17679, bubble stem. **$15-25**.

Balmoral #17711, bubble stem. **$15-25**.

Baroque #17666, bubble stem. **$15-25**.

Belle Meade #17660, platinum trim.
(Known as Patricia with gold trim.) **$15-25**.

Biarritz #17715. **$15-25**.

Blenheim #17301. **$15-25**.

Bolero #17598. **$15-25**.

Brisbane #17589, bubble stem. **$15-25**.
Caresse #17453. **$15-25**.

Buckingham #17507. **$20-30**.
Caribbean #17687. **$15-25**.

Candlelight #17669. **$15-25**.
Chanel #17596, bubble stem. **$15-25**.

Capri #17640, bubble stem. **$15-25**.
Chardonnay #17683. **$15-25**.

53

Chardonnay #17683: Goblet, Wine, Champagne/Sherbet, Ice Tea. **$15-25** each.
Cinderella #17453. **$15-25**.   Circe #17669. **$15-25**.

Chatham #17301. **$15-25**.
Clinton #17651. **$15-25**.

Chilton #17574. **$15-25**.
Cloverleaf #17453. **$15-25**.

Concerto #17673. **$15-25**.   Constance #17646. **$15-25**.   Courtship #17453. **$15-25**.   Daphne #17524. **$15-25**.

Deauville #17711, bubble stem. **$15-25**.   Desire #17646. **$15-25**.   Duke #17371. **$20-30**.   Dulce #17680. **$15-25**.

55

Top left: Elinor #17507. **$15-25.**

Top center: Elizabeth #17453, produced in the 1940s; a different Elizabeth cutting on stemline #17726 was produced during the late 1970s. Other pattern names were duplicated, yet were different cuttings, and appeared on different stemlines. **$15-25.**

Top right: Elizabeth #17726, bubble stem: Goblet, Wine, Champagne/Sherbet, Ice Tea. **$15-25** each.

Bottom left: Elizabeth #17726, bubble stem, produced late 1970s. **$15-25.**

Bottom center: Elyse #17683: Goblet, Wine, Champagne/Sherbet, Ice Tea. **$15-25** each.

Bottom right: 1960s advertisement featuring the Elyse cutting.

INTRACOMPANY CORRESPONDENCE

INTERPACE
CORPORATION

DATE Tiffin/December 21, 1970

TO Joe Maxwell   Irene Betz
    Don West   Mary Miller
    Charles Feasel   Lottie Heck
    Anita Nusbaum   Della Fowler
    William Wolf   Betty Barlekamp

SUBJ: NEW PRODUCT LABELS

1)   Franciscan Masterpiece Crystal with imprinted pattern names (with self-adhesive on printed surface/ face down on backing) To be applied on all Franciscan "A" patterns stemware which include the Villeroy & Boch. Adhere on bottom of base to read through from above.

2)   Franciscan Masterpiece Crystal (without pattern names) To be applied to Villeroy & Boch gift items; cut compotes, Palais Versailles accessories and all "B" pattern stemware.

3) Franciscan Crystal - Madeira
    To be applied only to the six shapes in the Madeira Crystal Casual Line/all colors.

4) Franciscan Crystal.(without name)
    To be applied to all items other than above; i.e., Canterbury gifts, etc.

We should have all of the new labels on hand from the supplier and all regular-line items should be labeled with one of the four labels described above. If there are any questions, please let me know.

C. W. Carlson,Jr.

CWC:mz

cc: C. F. Assenheimer

December 21, 1970, interoffice memo discussing how the various Franciscan Crystal labels are to be used.

Top center: Elmwood #17596, bubble stem. **$15-25**.

Top right: Embassy #17301. **$15-25**.

Bottom center: Enchantment #17640. **$15-25**.

Bottom right: Essex #17679, bubble stem. This cutting was previously known as Empire, renamed by Towle as Essex. **$15-25**.

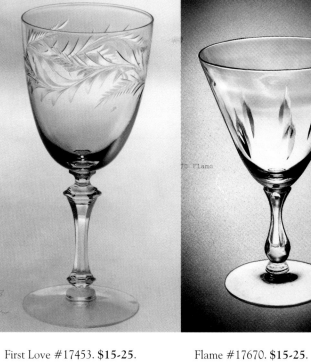

Fair Lady #17674. **$15-25**.

Fantasy #17566. **$15-25**.

Felicia #17674. **$15-25**.

First Love #17453. **$15-25**.

Flame #17670. **$15-25**.

Folia #17669. **$15-25**.

Forever #17453. **$15-25**.

Forever Yours #17507, introduced 1951. **$15-25**.

Frozen Fire #17688. **$15-25**.

Garland #17505, introduced 1951. **$15-25**.

Georgette #17700, Belvedere #17700. **$15-25** each.   Glen Auldyn #17660. **$15-25**.

Golden Image #17594, bubble
stem, gold trim. **$20-30**.

Golden Wheat
Crystal #17566 Goblets with gold inlay. **$25-35** each.

Bottom left: Harmony #17646. **$15-25**.

Bottom center: Harvest #17453, produced 1940s. **$15-25**.

Bottom right: Horizon #17665. **$15-25**.

59

Top left: Idyllic #17665. **$15-25**.

Top center: Interlude #17726, bubble stem, platinum trim. **$15-25**.

Top right: Interlude #17726, bubble stem: Goblet, Wine, Champagne/
    Sherbet, Ice Tea. **$15-25** each.

Bottom left: Intrigue #17651. **$15-25**.

Bottom center: Iris #17566, introduced in 1953. **$15-25**.

Bottom right: Jupiter #17477, gold or platinum inlay, introduced in 1953.
    $25-35.

Above: Jupiter Crystal #17477 Wines, with gold inlay. **$25-35** each.

Top row, left to right: Kristina #17675, bubble stem. **$15-25**.
Lady Carol #17524. **$15-25**.
Laureate #17665. **$15-25**.
Lenox Glendale #17601, bubble stem. **$20-30**.
Lady Hilton Crystal #W-1 Goblet, made for Nancy Prentiss. **$15-25**.

Bottom row, left to right: Lady Love #17651. **$15-25**.
Lenox Wreath #17418. **$15-25**.
Lilt #17565. **$15-25**.
Lisette #17684; Lyndley #17646, platinum trim (known as
  Provincial with gold trim). **$15-25** each.

Loraine #17665. **$15-25**.

Lorie #17670. **$15-25**.

Malibu #17566. **$15-25**.

Marcella #17594, bubble stem. **$15-25**.

Mariposa #17507, introduced in 1951. **$20-30**.

Marquis #17687; Melissa #17687. **$15-25** each.

Mayfair #17525. **$15-25**.

Melissa #17687, Goblet, Wine, Champagne/Sherbet, Ice Tea. **$15-25** each.

Mesa #17566, gray or polished cutting. **$15-25**.

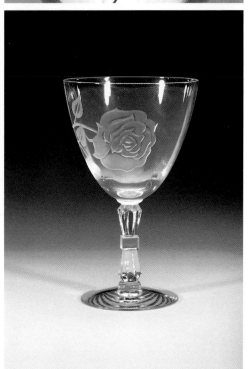

Top left: Mesa, Baroque
Crystal #17576 Ice Tea, gold inlay; #17566 Goblet, gold inlay. **$25-35** each.

Top center: Detail of Mesa engraving with gold inlay and enameled highlights.

Top right: Detail of Baroque with gold inlay.

Bottom left: Milburn Rose
Crystal #W-2 Goblet, made for Nancy Prentiss. **$15-25**.

Bottom right: Crystal #17546 Goblet, sand-carved "Rose" design. **$30-40**.

Mirage #17594,
bubble stem. **$15-25**.

Musette #17670. **$15-25**.

Ondine #17708: Goblet, Wine, Champagne/Sherbet, Ice Tea. **$20-30** each.

Pamela #17680. **$15-25**.

Parkwood
Crystal #17377 Goblet, bubble stem. Very popular
Tiffin cutting. **$30-40**.

Parkwood
Crystal #17377: Champagne, **$25-35**; Wine, **$30-40**; Goblet, **$30-40**; Cocktail, **$25-35**; Ice Tea, **$25-35**; all with bubble stem.

Parasienne #17670. **$15-25**.

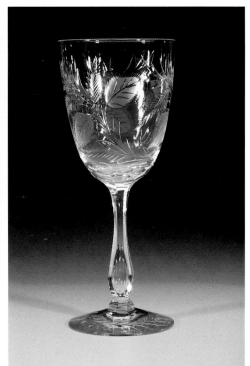

Parkwood
Crystal 9" 2-Lite Candelabrum, undocumented line number. **$100-125** pair.

Parkwood
Crystal #6462, 12" Cellini Bowl. **$250-300**.

Peer Gynt #17358. **$15-25**.

Perfection #17693, platinum trim. **$15-25**.

Phyllis #17359. **$15-25**.

July 19, 1940, patent record for the #17359 stemline, designed by Charles W. Carlson.

July 19, 1940, patent record for the #17371 stemline, designed by Charles W. Carlson.

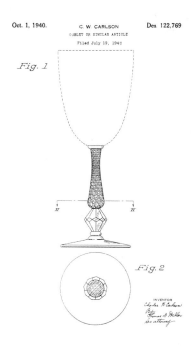

Pine Tree #17474. $25-35.

Pine Trio #17576, introduced in 1951. $15-25.

Pomona #17507. $20-30.

Priscilla #17361. $15-25.

Pristine #17442: Champagne/Sherbet, $10-20; Wine, $15-25; Goblet, $15-25; Ice Tea, $15-25; Cocktail, $10-20; Cordial, $25-35; Salad Plate, $8-12.

Promise #17651, introduced in 1951. $15-25.

17442 Pristine (Round foot)

66

Reflections #17683. **$15-25**.

Renaissance #17594, bubble stem.
$15-25.

Regency #17594, bubble stem, gold
trim and inlay. **$55-65**.

Rhapsody #17651. **$15-25**.

Regent #17394, produced 1940s.
$15-25.

Rhodora #17670. **$15-25**.

Regent
Crystal #17679 Goblet and Cordial, bubble stem with gold inlay.
Produced 1950s. **$40-$50**; **$60-70**.

Rose Marie #17501: Cocktail, **$10-20**; Champagne/Sherbet, **$10-20**; Goblet, **$15-25**; Ice Tea, **$15-25**.

Royal Splendor #17679, bubble stem. Very popular cutting. **$25-35**.

Royal York #17503. **$15-25**.

Sandra #17651, gold trim. **$15-25**.

Savoy
Crystal #17646, gold trim: Champagne, Cordial, Goblet. **$10-20**; **$25-35**; **$15-25**.

Sheffield #17502. **$15-25**.

Silver Wheat #17453. **$15-25**.

Silver Wheat #17524. **$15-25.**

Silver Wheat #17540. (Known as Golden Wheat with gold inlay.) **$15-25.**

Silver Wheat #17542. (Known as Golden Wheat with gold inlay.) **$15-25.**

Silver Wheat #17546. **$15-25.**

Simplicity #17651. **$15-25.**

Skylark #17551, introduced in 1951. **$15-25.**

Sonja #17351. **$15-25.**

Spring Blossom #17651. **$15-25.**

Spring Song #17670, introduced in 1951. **$15-25.**

Spring Tide #17665. **$15-25.**

Squire #17553. **$15-25**.

Sylvia #17669, platinum trim. **$15-25**.

Starlight #17625: Goblet, **$15-25**; Wine, **$15-25**; Champagne/Sherbet, **$10-20**; Ice Tea, **$15-25**.

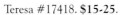

Teresa #17418. **$15-25**.

Theda #17546. **$15-25**.

Surf #17646, introduced in 1959. **$15-25**.

Surrey #17395. **$15-25**.

Theme #17644: Goblet, Wine, Champagne/Sherbet. **$15-25** each.

Tiara #17489. **$15-25**.

Triomphe #17594, bubble stem, gold trim. **$15-25**.

Tiara #17625, bubble stem, gold trim: Goblet, **$15-25**; Wine, **$15-25**; Champagne/Sherbet, **$10-20**; Ice Tea, **$15-25**.

Triomphe #17594, bubble stem, gold trim: Goblet, **$15-25**; Wine, **$15-25**; Champagne/Sherbet, **$10-20**; Ice Tea, **$15-25**.

Tivoli #17357. **$15-25**.

Truly Yours #17638, bubble stem. **$15-25**.

July 19, 1940, patent record for the #17357 stemline, designed by Charles W. Carlson.

Tudor #17507. **$20-30**.

Tudor #17507: Goblet, **$20-30**; Wine, **$20-30**; Champagne/Sherbet, **$15-25**; Ice Tea, **$20-30**.

Twilight #17690, platinum trim. **$15-25**.

Vespera #17669. **$15-25**.

Bottom row, left to right:
Vogue #17551. **$15-25**.
Warwick #17681. **$15-25**.
Weatherly #17670, platinum trim. **$15-25**.
Wellington #17623, bubble stem. **$15-25**.

White House #17671, with cut eagle; White House #17671, without eagle. The White House stem with the cut eagle was ordered by President Franklin Roosevelt in 1937 from T.G. Hawkes and Company of Corning, New York. T.G. Hawkes performed the cutting on blanks provided by the United States Glass Company from Factory R (Tiffin). President Roosevelt ordered sherrys, wines, goblets, champagnes, cordials, and finger bowls for his table service. The White House stem without the cut eagle was made available to the public in 1961 by the United States Glass Company. Goblets retailed for $78.00 per dozen. **$40-50**; **$25-35**.

Publicity photo showing table setting of White House crystal.

Windfall #17665. **$15-25**.   York #17651. **$15-25**.   Zinfandel #17711, bubble stem. **$15-25**.

Julie #17702, **$15-25**; Resplendent #17726, bubble stem, **$15-25**; Suzanne #17507, **$20-30**; Rosemary #17707, **$15-25**.

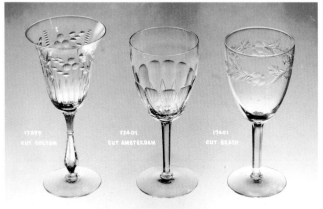

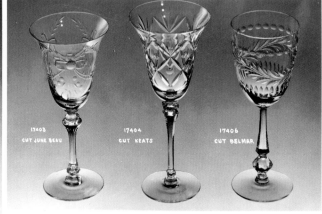

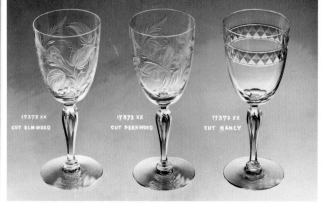

Top: Colton #17399; Amsterdam #17401; Heath #17401.
$15-25 each.
Bottom: Antwerp #17402, bubble stem; #17402 bubble stem;
Hillcrest #17403. **$15-25** each.

Top: Astrid #17372; Elegance #17372; Elegance #17372
(reverse view). All bubble stems. **$20-30** each.
Bottom: Elmwood #17372; Fernwood #17372; Nancy #17372.
All bubble stems. **$20-30**; **$20-30**; **$15-25**.

Top: June Beau #17403; Keats #17404; Belmar #17406.
$15-25 each.
Bottom: Brenda #17406; Bridal Knot #17406; Charlton
#17406. **$15-25** each.

74

Top: Florence #17361; Idylwide #17361; Laurel Wreath #17361. **$15-25** each.
Bottom: Mirabelle #17361; Priscilla #17361; Puritan #17361; Warwick #17361. **$15-25** each.

Top: #17397 cut stem; Adoration #17397; Ecstasy #17397. **$15-25** each.
Bottom: Mystic #17397; Tiger Lily #17397; Adoration #17399. **$15-25** each.

Top: Delys #17387; Paula #17391, bubble stem; Rotterdam #17391, bubble stem. **$15-25** each.

Bottom: Mystic #17378; Linda #17378; Londonderry #17378. **$20-30**; **$15-25**; **$15-25**.

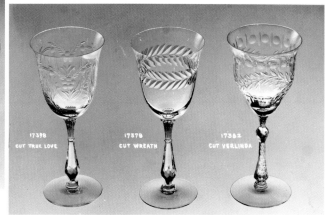

Top: Christian #17363; Paula #17363; Goteberg #17363. All bubble stems. **$15-25** each.
Bottom: Oxford #17363; St. Louis #17363; Tyra #17363. All bubble stems. **$15-25** each.

Top: Athlone #17347; Pembrooke #17347; Shelley #17347. **$15-25** each.
Bottom: Woodstock #17347; Viking #17348; Wreath #17348. **$15-25** each.

Top: Royalty #17377, bubble stem; Ankara #17378; Ferndale #17378. **$15-25** each.
Bottom: True Love #17398; Wreath #17378; Verlinda #17382. **$15-25** each.

76

Top: Ardsley #17358; Allegro #17358; Delys #17358. **$15-25** each.

Bottom: Radiant #17358; Adoration #17361; Astrid #17361. **$15-25** each.

Top: Spikes #17301; Wallingford #17301; Williamsburg #17301. **$15-25** each.
Bottom: Woodstock #17301; Parkwood #17311; Tulip #17311. **$15-25** each.

Top: Vera #14184; Kent #17301; Athlone #17301. **$15-25** each.
Bottom: Mayflower #17301; Mayflower #17301; Pembrooke #17301. **$15-25** each.

Top: Regent #17394; Bridal Band #17395; Canterbury #17395. **$15-25** each.
Bottom: Chippendale #17395; Jefferson #17395; Jefferson Flutes #17395. **$15-25** each.

Top: Fleurette #17406; Idylwilde #17406; Beaufort #17407. **$15-25** each.
Bottom: Concerto #17407; Surrette #17409; Falstaff #17433, bubble stem. **$15-25** each.

Top: Erin #17394; Liege #17394; Lord Nelson #17394. **$15-25** each.

Bottom left: #17551 stemline, unknown cutting. **$15-25**.

Bottom right: #17356 stemline, unknown cutting. **$15-25**.

Crystal #17358 Ice Tea, Wide Optic, Melrose etching, Melrose gold band; Old Fashion, undocumented line number and cutting; #17683 Ice Tea, Elyse cutting; all with ceramic feet, experimental pieces made in 1976. **$25-35**; **$15-25**; **$25-35**.

Bottom left: Crystal Goblet with cut prism stem, and "Cross" engraving. This was done by a glassworker on his own time, then given to an incoming clergyman. **$175-200**.

Bottom center: Crystal Wine and Cocktail, hexagonal base, undocumented cutting and line number, Paul Williams collection, attributed to Tiffin Glass. **$25-35** each.

Bottom right: Crystal Chalice with Smoke paperweight base and Ondine engraved bowl with gold inlay, made by Vincent Meier. These were made by glassworkers and given to incoming clergymen. **$175-200**.

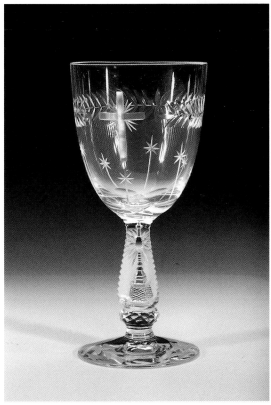

Tiffin

"VERLINDA" "LIEGE" "ELEGANCE"

TIFFIN LEADS IN RICH DIVERSITY OF DESIGN

From the hands of master craftsmen who know how to bring out all the beauty that lives in fine crystal. The trio of gracious designs pictured here symbolizes the far-flung scope of theme in the many new cuttings and shapes which Tiffin has just ushered into the market. Diversity of style and high quality of metal plus skillful workmanship—these join forces in a series of stemware designs which are keyed to the tastes of American hostesses of 1941.

United States Glass Company
Tiffin, Ohio

NEW YORK OFFICE
1107 Broadway

SAN FRANCISCO, CALIF.
308 Western Merchandise Mart

CHICAGO OFFICE
1573 Merchandise Mart

June Night   Sylvan   Marcia   Princess

Stemware By Tiffin

Fresh from the Hands of Tiffin Master Craftsmen

a new addition of designs in fine crystal, developed by artists who are keenly aware of the trends in American taste. Only a part of the story is told here — the complete collection includes about 40 carefully styled decorations on a varied group of shapes.

United States Glass Company
Tiffin, Ohio

NEW YORK OFFICE
1107 Broadway

SAN FRANCISCO, CALIF.
308 Western Merchandise Mart

CHICAGO OFFICE
1573 Merchandise Mart

magnificent table jewels...

...as seen regularly
in
House Beautiful
and
House & Garden

a tiffin creation:

united states glass company, tiffin, ohio

Top row, left to right:
February 1941 United States Glass Company advertisement from *China, Glass and Lamps.*

United States Glass Company advertisement from *China and Glass.*

Early 1940s advertisement by the United States Glass Company featuring the Priscilla cutting.

Bottom row, left to right:
Early 1940s advertisement by the United States Glass Company featuring the Antwerp and Elegance cuttings.

Early 1940s advertisement by the United States Glass Company featuring the Liege and Mystic cuttings.

April 1942 advertisement by the United States Glass Company from *China and Glass* featuring the Ecstasy cutting.

Early 1940s advertisement by the United States Glass Company featuring the Parkwood cutting.

precious Jewels
of tiffin

...as seen regularly
in
House Beautiful
and
House & Garden

united states glass company, tiffin, ohio

Coveted Jewels
by tiffin

...as seen regularly
in
House Beautiful
and
House & Garden

united states glass company, tiffin, ohio

For the Hostess-to-Be...

As the June bridal season approaches, the demand for Tiffin stemware becomes more pronounced. The sheer loveliness . . . the superb quality . . . and the unsurpassed craftsmanship of these Tiffin creations have made them the preference of America's discriminating hostesses, present and future. Suggest Tiffin stemware as the ideal bridal gift.

No. 17397 Cut "Ecstasy"

United States Glass Company
Tiffin, Ohio

NEW YORK OFFICE
1107 Broadway

LOS ANGELES, CALIF.
712 South Olive Street

CHICAGO OFFICE
1573 Merchandise Mart

Entered as second class matter at the Post Office in Pittsburgh on November 18, 1909, under the Act of March 3, 1879
Published each month by the Commoner Publishing Co., Seventh Street, Pittsburgh, Pa. Subscription Price $2.00 the year
CHINA AND GLASS   VOL. 41.   No. 8.   APRIL, 1942.

Jewel of flawless beauty
by tiffin

...as seen regularly
in
House Beautiful
and
House & Garden

united states glass company . . . tiffin, ohio

Reprint of advertisement appearing in:
Bride's Magazine and Modern Bride, Fall 1956

1956 United States Glass Company advertisement featuring the LaRue and Dawn cuttings.

Top right: Late 1950s United States Glass Company advertisement.

Bottom right: Late 1950s United States Glass Company advertisement.

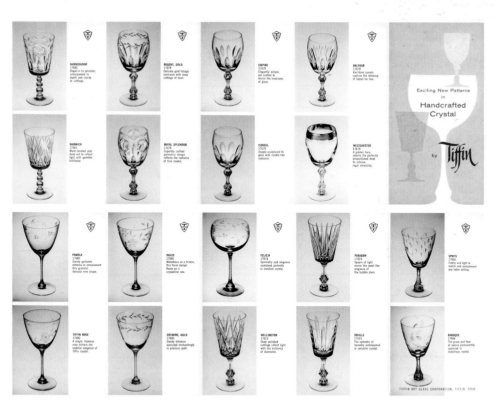

1964 Tiffin Art Glass Corporation pamphlet showing popular patterns offered at that time.

Early 1980 advertisement, one of the last advertisements produced before the furnaces were shut down in May 1980.

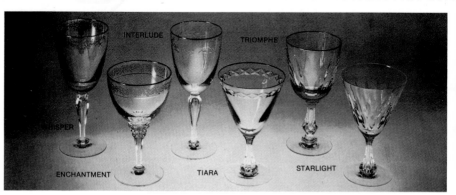

82

Top left: Early 1980 Towle Silversmiths advertisement.

Top center: Early 1980 Towle Silversmiths advertisement.

Top right: Unidentified woman shown marking designs on stemware to be cut later.

Bottom left: Photograph of unidentified man stripping the lehr in the finishing department.

Bottom right: Della Fowler inspecting stemware in the finishing department.

83

1967 photograph of part of the interior of the Tiffin Glass outlet store.

1967 interior shot of the Tiffin Glass outlet store, Joan Rahrig behind the counter. Some of the items on the shelving are remainders from prior years.

The name "Tiffin" used as a back-stamp on every stem assures your customers that they are investing in America's Prestige Crystal.

WILLIAMSBURG
17301
Brilliant geometric colonial cutting is timeless in its appeal.

EDINBURGH
17440
Notable: the diamond-cut base, a footnote to the pattern's elegance.

DOLORES
17453
The graceful cutting complements the trend to china border patterns.

3

Tiffin
Rose

Shown here are the graceful goblet, champagne-sherbet and claret . . . three most desired stems, in the wondrously graceful rose pattern which has become synonymous with the name Tiffin.

PALAIS VERSAILLES (GOLD)
17594
The highest form of elegance in crystal . . . lavishly gold-lighted.

MINTON (GOLD)
17601
Intricately cut stem echoes the widely serrated luxury of gold.

PARAGON
17623
Reflective sunburst effect will flood a table with brilliance.

SHAPE 17623	

5

FESTIVAL
17640
Polished cuttings circling bowl, and elegance in the bubble stem.

THEME
17644
A shower of graceful cuttings . . combining delicacy with richness.

CARILLON (PLATINUM) SAVOY (GOLD)
17646
Delicately curved floral motif accents many fine china patterns.

KENT (PLATINUM)
17646
Perfectly proportioned to be embellished by only a gleaming band.

LYNDLEY (PLATINUM)
17646
A stem of extraordinary dignity, to be highly prized for a lifetime.

CLINTON
17651
Rows of deeply-polished cuttings capture lights in every facet.

SHAPE 17646	

7

The 1967 catalog consists of a selection of the most popular designs that were offered at that time by the Tiffin Glass Company. Platinum and gold bands were used extensively on blanks and cut stemware. No plate etchings were offered.

BROOKMAR (PLATINUM)
17477
A fine example of the simplicity so revealing of Tiffin's quality.

PETITE
17524
Gay and witty cutting, designed especially for the young in heart.

MARGO
17524
Slender cuttings pirouette atop a stem of gem-brilliant facets.

LINDA
17576
Popular leaf spray, as shown, or with spray and a rich gold band.

BLAIR HOUSE
17594
Destined to become a cherished heirloom of lustrous grandeur.

MIRAGE
17594
Six mirror-like oval panties that gleam above the rich bubble stem.

SHAPE 17594	

4

Tiffin
Cara Mia

The charm of a beautifully appointed table is apparent at the very start of the first course, when the setting includes the inevitable goblet . . . plus the champagne-sherbet counterpointed against the clarity of the crystal plate. All shown here in Tiffin's Cara Mia pattern.

WELLINGTON
17623
Deep polished cuttings . . . as only Tiffin craftsmanship achieves.

FAIRFAX (PLATINUM)
17638
Always in good taste . . Tiffin's highly traditional Grail shape.

DELITE (PLATINUM) MANSFIELD (GOLD)
17640
Narrow-banded . . to accent fully the sparkle of true leaded crystal.

SHAPE 17640	

6

MONTCLAIR (PLATINUM) STRAUSBOURG (GOLD)
17651
Exquisite handmade lead crystal from pedestal to gleaming rim.

CAPRICE (PLATINUM) MERCEDES (GOLD)
17657
The sought-for simplicity which is versatile for any table mood.

ARGENTA (PLATINUM)
17660
A touch of grace in the stem, to cradle the brilliance of the bowl.

HEIRLOOM (PLATINUM) CASCADE (GOLD)
17651
The hand-applied band is a symbol of Tiffin skill and craftsmanship.

OAKLAWN
17664
Cuttings at the base of the bowl add subtle brilliance to the table.

CAMELOT
17665
Equally suitable for a table in a castle . . . or a smart American home.

SHAPE 17651	

8

**CARA MIA (PLATINUM)
GOLCONDA (GOLD)
17665**
A Tiffin star . . . please see Page 6 for a lovely Cara Mia grouping.

**WALES
17665**
Hand-cut floral design creates a crystal jewel for tables to wear.

**TEMPLE
17666**
The popular "teardrop" bubble stem appears to reflect the rich cutting.

Tiffin Manchester

Amenable to a variety of decorative treatments from very simple to stunningly elaborate, the Tiffin shape 17679 is fast becoming an American classic. It is never more beautiful than in the Manchester decoration. Note particularly the grace of the highly prized iced tea glass.

Tiffin Elyse

An outstandingly beautiful example of Tiffin's modern revival of motifs most sought after during the golden era of cut glass in America: the Brilliant Period. In perfect taste for generations to come, as well.

**HUNTINGTON
17685**
Contemporary? Traditional? The shape and decor are as you use it.

**CARLYLE
17685**
Double prisms, graceful form . . . to be prized for its heritage value.

**ARLINGTON
17685**
Multi-faceted, to gleam with the brilliance of a crystal chandelier.

Brides-to-be

. . . hear the Tiffin story, see the beauty of Tiffin patterns, learn about our Pattern Replacement Program . . . through ads in magazines that are avidly read by the girls in this huge market. They will be your customers!

**THAYMORE
17666**
From a tradition of English folk-lore . . this sheerly elegant pattern.

CLASSIC (PLATINUM)
The continental shape now so much favored, handed to the modern mood.

**WESTCHESTER (GOLD)
17679**
The decorated gold tiara crowns a perfectly proportioned bowl.

**WIND SONG (PLATINUM)
FLORENTINE (GOLD)
17679**
With simple banding, the total beauty of this shape is apparent.

**TIFFIN ROSE
17680**
A single rose, named for us alone . . . and worthy of the name.

**MOONSTONE
17684**
Star-traced fantasy in this dainty yet most luxurious Tiffin cutting.

**JULIE
17684**
A graceful sweep, destined for harmony with many new china patterns.

**LISETTE
17684**
Brilliant flame-cut prisms at the bowl-base for a mood of elegance.

Please Remember . . .

Tiffin's fabulous Pattern Replacement Program is the "plus" that is yours with all of these new Modern Brilliant patterns. This is particularly important for the series presented here, because they are certainly destined to become family heirlooms, and it pleases customers to know that they can always get replacements for breakage . . . or that a pattern will always be available to add to originally purchased settings.

SHAPE 17665							

9

SHAPE 17664 (as seen on Page 6)							

13

SHAPE 17683							

15

SHAPE 17685							

17

**BALFOUR
17679**
Reminiscent of the baguette-cut in jewels, and equally as sparkling.

**CONSUL
17679**
A bowl-shape that lends itself well to elaborate cutting, as seen here.

**EMPIRE
17679**
In the elaborate mood of Empire design, a pattern of great dignity.

**ELEGANCE
17682**
Sparkling and darting with fire-lit, highly polished hand cutting.

**SUSSEX
17682**
An heirloom shape of timeless proportions, cut for lasting beauty.

**WILLOW
D-3**
Like a shower of small diamond spray flowers caught in crystal.

Tiffin Carlyle

A pattern of such elegant brilliance that it becomes the conversation-center of any table . . . always at home, in settings modern or traditional . . . always an eloquent compliment to the hostess who chooses it.

Plan a Tiffin "Crystal Wardrobe" For and With Your Customers

Because of our Permanent Pattern Replacement Program, it is well to impress your customers that Tiffin fine crystal is a long-term investment . . . one that can become a family heritage.

Once they start a Tiffin crystal service, they need never think in terms of buying any more "sets" for the rest of their lives, because their Tiffin can always be replaced, should breakage occur . . . and more pieces can always be added. A mighty nice savings through the years!

Start your customer with 8's or 12's in: goblets, champagne - sherbets, clarets . . . these three items are ample to set a table to be proud of.

The Tiffin Permanent Pattern Replacement Program: How It Can Work For You

You are, of course, familiar with the "open stock" arrangement prevalent in table appointments. Tiffin IS "open stock" . . . but our plan for flexibility in supply to a customer goes far beyond this.

Tiffin crystal plates and cordials or iced teas should become the next investment.

With all stemware shapes and patterns registered and on file at the Tiffin factories, it is quite possible for us to reach back into history and pull out the most obsolete of Tiffin patterns for the purpose of making a limited re-run. This is exactly what we do under our Permanent Pattern Replacement Program.

For you, the Tiffin Permanent Pattern Replacement Program serves two purposes.

First, you can sell more easily, since you have the powerful benefit to the customer of stating that her Tiffin pattern will always be available . . . it is a permanent pattern. That is why we say, "Tiffin is Forever."

Second, you assure yourself of repeat sales, extra volume every year when you announce the Tiffin Permanent Pattern Replacement Program.

Follow with juice glasses, cocktails, dessert nappies, finger bowls and the other Tiffin specialties that become the most brilliant conversationalists at any dinner table.

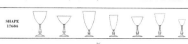

**MANCHESTER
17679**
Most cherished of all patterns on this exquisite Tiffin shape.

**ROMA, GOLD
17679**
Reflecting the high demand for a gold band of classic derivation.

**ROYAL SPLENDOR
17679**
Superbly crafted geometric design reflects the radiance of true crystal.

**ELYSE
17683**
Most popular pattern in Tiffin's favored Modern Brilliant series.

**KEEPSAKE, PLATINUM
17684**
All brilliance and light . . . with a platinum band to add to its grace.

**MORNING ROSE
17684**
The dewy freshness of early morn . . . in this version of the Tiffin Rose.

**WOODMERE
17684**
For versatility and harmony; this rich combination of prism and scroll.

**BELFAST
17684**
Double rows of prisms, gracefully spaced, for the opulent new look.

**NEWCASTLE
17684**
Prisms and cross-cuttings . . . true heralds of the Brilliant Period.

SHAPE 17679							

12

SHAPE 17682							

14

SHAPE 17684							

16

18

Chapter 4
Blown Colored Ware

The majority of the blown colored ware included in this volume was produced from 1948 through 1955. Limited color production took place in the 1960s and 1970s. Few tableware accessory items were offered. Although the majority of the stemware was not decorated, a minimal amount was embellished with gold, platinum, plate etchings, and cuttings, particularly Killarney items.

Killarney with Crystal trim #17394 Goblet, gold band. **$50-70**.

Killarney with Crystal trim and sterling silver base, #17394: Goblet, Wine, and Champagne. **$45-65** each.

Killarney with Crystal trim: #6233, 2 qt. Jug; #17674 Goblets, one with gold encrusted Minton band, c. 1950. **$275-300**; **$40-50**; **$30-40**.

Killarney with Crystal trim: #6021 Seafood Cocktail with Crystal liner, **$50-70**; #17394 Goblet, **$20-30**; Footed Juice, **$15-25**; Ice Tea, **$15-25**; Cordial, **$40-50**; Champagne, **$15-25**; #6244, 3 ½" h. Cigarette Holder, **$45-65**; all produced in 1948.

Killarney
Killarney with Crystal trim #15074: Whiskey Sour, **$30-40**;
Cordial, **$50-60**; Goblet, **$25-35**; Wine, **$25-35**; Champagne,
$20-30; all produced in 1948.

Top left: Shamrock
Killarney with Crystal trim #17458: Ice
Tea, **$15-25**; Footed Tumbler, **$15-25**;
Champagne, **$15-25**; Cordial, **$40-$50**;
Goblet, **$20-30**; Wine, **$20-30**; all produced
in 1948.

Top right: Shamrock
Killarney with Crystal trim #17665 Sherry.
$40-$50.

Bottom left: Killarney with Crystal trim:
#17405 Seafood Cocktail, **$25-35**;
#17450 Cocktail, **$20-30**; #17471
Sundae, **$20-30**; all produced in 1948.

Bottom right: Killarney with Crystal trim,
#17430 Cigarette Server, Tumblers,
produced in 1948. **$35-45** each.

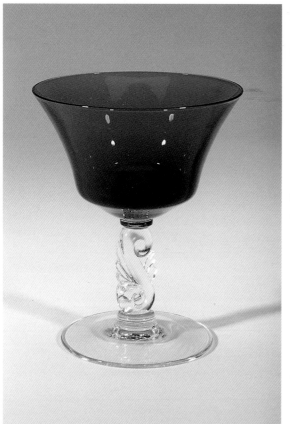

Top left: Minton Green
Killarney with Crystal trim #17394 Goblet, Minton gold band. **$50-70.**

Top center: Killarney with Crystal trim #17450 Goblet and Champagne. **$30-40; $25-35.**

Bottom left: Dolphin
Killarney with Crystal trim #17468 Champagne. **$25-35.**

Bottom right: September 1949 United States Glass Company advertisement from *Crockery and Glass Journal* featuring Killarney tableware.

There are no words to describe Wistaria truly. Its color a cross of rose, blue and starlight. Its brilliance fiery . . . its transparency complete. There's laughter in it . . it changes at all levels, in all lights. To the bride it's the new . . the prized never-before. To the sophisticate, tomorrow's big drama. To the traditionalist, it was always missing until now. To the decorator, theme for the most brilliant table settings ever made. The accomplishment, a new great in the history of glass; sparkling color transparency in crystal. Color to see through. Color to catch and play with light. Color to go with everything . . . and make everything lovelier for it. Water plays a trick in it . . . forming a "halo" at its crest in the glass! Priced for all, at the fine stores listed opposite. Hand-blown, hand-shaped new masterpiece by

Wistaria

by The Tiffin Glassmasters

The Tiffin Glassmasters
TIFFIN, OHIO

Better Homes & Gardens magazine October 1950 advertisement by the United States Glass Company promoting Wistaria and the Tiffin Glassmasters.

Wistaria with Crystal trim #17505 Goblet. $30-40.

Wistaria with Crystal trim #17501 Goblet. $30-40.

Wistaria with Crystal trim #17501: Goblet, $30-40; Wine, $30-40; Cordial, $50-60; Ice Tea, $25-35; Claret, $30-40.

Pink Rain
Wistaria with Crystal trim #17477: Goblet, Champagne, Wine, Ice Tea, $40-50 each; Wistaria #8833, 8" Plate, $20-25. Also produced on the #17551 stemline.

Syncapation
Wistaria with Crystal trim
#17477 Cocktails. **$20-30**
each.

Top: Wistaria with Crystal trim #17507: Wine, **$30-40**; Goblet, **$30-40**; Champagne, **$25-35**; Ice Tea, **$25-35**; Cordial, **$50-60**.

Bottom: Wistaria with Crystal trim #17658 Holiday Tumblers. **$40-$50** each.

Wistaria with Crystal trim #17477: Champagne, **$20-30**; Goblet, **$25-35**; Cocktail, **$25-35**; Wine, **$25-35**.

Left: Wistaria with Crystal trim #17507 Goblet. **$30-40**.

Right: Carmel Wistaria with Crystal trim #17477: Goblet and Champagne. **$35-45**; **$30-40**. Wistaria #8833, 8" Plate, **$15-20**. All items with platinum trim.

Left: Wistaria with Crystal trim #17477 Goblet. **$25-35**.

Right: Wistaria with Crystal trim #17394: Goblet, Cordial, Champagne. **$20-30**; **$50-60**; **$15-25**.

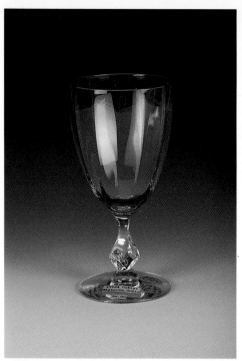
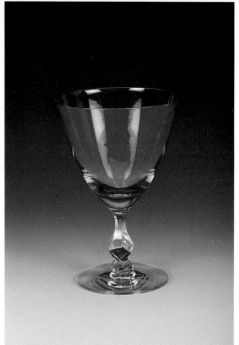
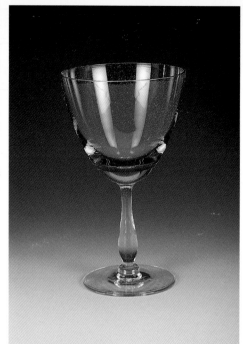

Top row, left to right:
Wistaria with Crystal trim #17524 Goblet, Wide Optic. **$30-40.**

Wistaria with Crystal trim #17525 Goblet. **$30-40.**

Wistaria with Crystal trim #17551 Goblet. **$30-40.**

Cherry Blossom #17477 Goblet, satin finish; Wistaria with Crystal trim #17477 Cordial. The Cherry Blossom goblet, produced in 1956, has a pale pink bowl, as opposed to the Wistaria color. **$30-40; $50-60.**

Bottom: Lenox Rose
Azalea #17376-2: Goblet, **$35-45**; Champagne, **$30-40**; Ice tea, **$30-40**; Cocktail, **$30-40**; Wine, **$35-45**; all Wide Optic and sand carved.

Opposite page, *top left:*
Carnation #17566 Goblet, **$25-35.** This same shade of pink was identified under different names depending upon the stemline: Azalea, #17576; Carnation, #17566; Cherry Blossom, #17477; Wild Rose, #17606. These were produced in 1956.

(See opposite page for caption.)

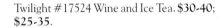

Twilight #17525: Champagne, **$25-35**; Wine, **$30-40**; Ice Tea, **$25-35**; Goblet, **$30-40**.

Twilight #17525 Goblet. **$30-40**.

Twilight #17525 Goblet with gold encrusted Minton band. **$50-60**.

Twilight #17524 Wine and Ice Tea. **$30-40**; **$25-35**.

Twilight #17524 Goblet. **$30-40**.

Twilight #17507, Wide Optic, Goblet. **$40-$50**.

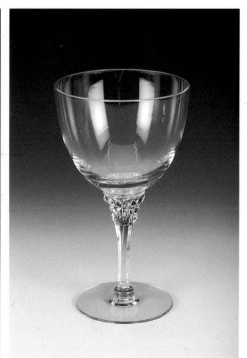

Parkwood
Twilight #17492 Goblet,
limited production. **$50-65**.

Twilight #17530 Goblet.
$25-35.

Twilight #17578 Goblet
and Champagne. **$35-45**;
$30-40.

Twilight #17573 Holiday Tumbler. Two
other sizes of tumblers were also produced.
$40-$50.

Twilight #17581 Goblet, bubble stem.
$35-45.

Minton Twilight
Twilight #17507 Goblet, Minton gold band, Wide Optic. **$65-90**.

Flambeau
Twilight #17722, Wide Optic: Tumbler, **$25-35**; Juice/Wine, **$25-35**; Sherbet, **$20-30**; Ice Tea, **$25-35**; produced circa 1978. A goblet and an on the rocks were also made.

Pink, Twilight #17702 Goblets with "Enameled Rings," limited production, c. late 1970s. **$30-40**; **$35-45**.

Flambeau
Evening Sun #17722 Goblets. **$10-20** each. In the Flambeau line, the Golden Banana color is called Evening Sun.

Cobalt Blue with Crystal trim #17662 Champagnes, c.1961. **$30-40** each.

Bottom left: Cobalt Blue with Crystal trim #17679 Goblet. **$35-45**.

Top right: Cobalt Blue with Crystal trim #17685 Goblet and Champagne. **$35-45**; **$30-40**.

Bottom right: Twilight #17722 Goblet, Flambeau line, **$20-25**; Plum with Crystal trim, Ice Tea, undocumented line number, Alfresco line, **$15-20**. The Flambeau and Alfresco lines are very similar in appearance. The Alfresco foot has a series of ridges that extend up the stem, while the Flambeau foot is smooth.

Smoke with Crystal trim: #17392 Champagne, Wide Optic; #17679 Goblet, bubble stem; #17679 Champagne; #17665 Champagne. This photo shows the variation in Smoke color. **$10-20** each.

Indigo
Smoke #17688 Goblet and Cordial with encrusted platinum band. **$15-25**; **$25-35**.

Detail of platinum band.

Dusk
Smoke #17690 Goblet and Champagne. **$10-20** each.

Top center: Plum with Smoke trim: #17693 Champagne; #17688 Goblets, very limited production. **$20-30** each.

Top right: Desert Red with Crystal trim #17524 Wines, c.1970. **$15-25** each.

Top: Plum with Crystal trim: #17680 Wine and #17693 Goblets. **$15-25** each.

Bottom: Plum #453, 9 oz. Old Fashion Cocktail; #17580, 9 oz. Old Fashion; both Diamond Optic, 1961. **$15-25** each.

Winter Green #17657 Champagne. **$20-25**. Discontinued in May 1962.

"Aqua" #17707 Toasting Goblets. **$75-100**.

"Green" #14196 Goblet; Lagoon #17702 Goblet; both with "Red Enameled Rings," limited production, c.late 1970s. **$30-40** each.

"Green" #17597 Champagne, bubble stem. **$20-30**.

Golden Banana with Crystal trim #17683 Champagne and Goblet; very limited production. **$10-20**; **$15-25**.

#17683 Goblets: Golden Banana with Crystal trim, Crystal with Smoke trim, Pink with Crystal trim. **$15-25** each.

Crystal with Smoke trim #17594 Wine; Crystal with Golden Banana trim #17594 Goblet: both with bubble stem. **$15-25** each.

Below: Greenbriar with Crystal trim #17693 Ice Teas: Plum Wines, Champagne, undocumented line number. **$10-20** each.

Golden Banana #17662 Ice Teas. **$15-25** each.

Top left: Flame with Crystal trim Ice Teas, undocumented line number, c.1960. **$35-45** each.

Top right: Flame with Black trim #17696 Goblet; Flame with Smoke trim #17702 Goblet, very limited production. **$35-45** each.

Flame with Crystal trim #17667 Toasting Goblets with Flame chain. **$125-150**.

Crystal #17433 Cocktail and Cordial, **$10-20**; **$15-20**. Crystal #17659 with Desert Red trim, **$15-20**; Golden Banana #6125, 4 ¾" h. Candle Holder, **$35-50**; all items with bubble stem. Note that the candle holder has the same shape of stem as the stemware.

Ebony
Black #17657 Goblets. **$10-20** each; Black #17703 Goblet, Cordial, Champagne/
Sherbet, made for American Manor. **$10-20**; **$20-30**; **$10-15**.

Midnight Halo
Black #17710: Ice Tea, **$10-20**; Cordial, **$20-30**; Goblet, **$10-20**; Wine,
$10-20; Champagne/Sherbet, **$10-15**; Table Bell, **$15-25**; made for
Reynolds Crystal.

. . . . In fact that's one of the problems we have with it. It cools too fast! Especially so when we're creating a pattern like this with its long delicate stem.

In our more than 75 years of producing America's most outstanding lead crystal we have never worked with a color that presented such unique beauty . . . . and such unique challenges.

Of course all fine lead crystal has minor bubbles, cords, and sheer marks. And in black the color tends to magnify these.

They are still considered normal and acceptable though and are to be found in all black crystal now being produced by any manufacturer.

In spite of this we think you'll agree our new black pattern is the most exciting crystal on the market today and one that will bring raves from your guests each time you entertain.

black is cool....

AMERICAN MANOR
LEAD CRYSTAL

INTERPACE
CORPORATION

Interpace pamphlet, c.1974.

Black #17710 Toasting Goblets. **$50-75**.

Black #17701 Goblets, with bright and satin finishes. **$10-20** each.

Black with Crystal trim #17609 Goblet, bubble stem. **$15-25**.

Persian Brocade.
Black #17709: Ice Tea, **$10-20**; Cordial, **$20-30**; Footed Tumbler, **$10-15**; Juice, **$10-15**; 6 ½" h. Candlesticks, undocumented line number, **$35-45** pair, made for Salad Master.

Crystal #17358 Goblets with undocumented floral enameling, very limited production. $40-$50 each.

Top: Crystal #17402 Goblet with blue filament stem. One of two known filament stems produced at the Tiffin factory. A red filament stem is documented on the #15082 stemline. **$65-85**.

Bottom: Midnight Mist #17690 platinum trim: Goblet, Wine, Champagne/Sherbet, Ice Tea. Midnight Mist was produced on Smoke blanks. **$15-25** each.

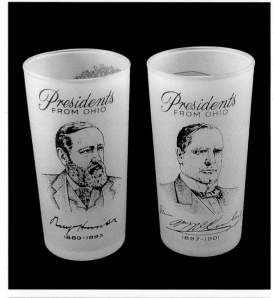

Top: Crystal Satin Tumblers with decals of President Benjamin Harrison and President William McKinley. A series of eight tumblers were produced honoring the U.S. Presidents from the state of Ohio. These were produced for the Meadow Gold Dairy in Tiffin, Ohio, as cottage cheese containers. **$10-15** each.

Bottom: Reverse side of tumblers showing the homes of President Harrison and President McKinley.

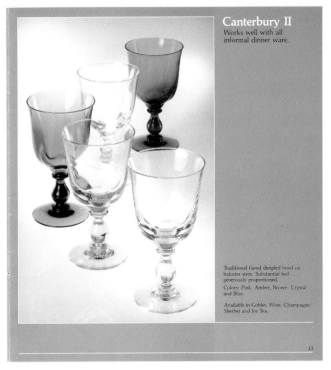

Canterbury II #17723. Canterbury II was introduced in 1978 in several colors on four sizes of stems. Canterbury II was not produced from Duncan Miller Glass Company molds; it was originated by the Tiffin Glass Company. The photo designates the pattern as Canterbury; however, the actual name is Canterbury II. The price for Crystal stems would range from **$5-10**; for colored stems, add an additional 50%.

1979 pamphlet showing the Canterbury II design.

Jubilation #17707. The Jubilation line was introduced circa 1978 in four sizes of stems. Prices range from **$5-10** for Crystal, 50% additional for colored stems.

Celestial #17707. Made for American Manor. **$10-15** each.

Revelation #17702. The Revelation line was introduced circa 1978 in four sizes of stems. Prices range from **$10-15** for colored stems.

Chantilly #17702. Made for American Manor. **$10-15** each.

1979 pamphlet showing the #17702 Revelation stemline.

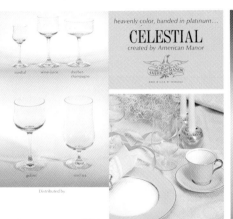

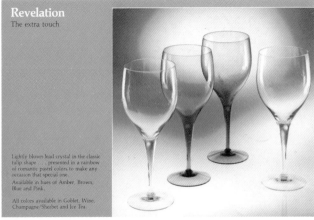

Chapter 5
Named and Plain Blanks

Many examples included in this chapter are simple designs identified by line number only. In most cases, decorations are limited to gold or platinum bands; no cuttings are included.

Carlton #17549, platinum trim. **$15-25**.

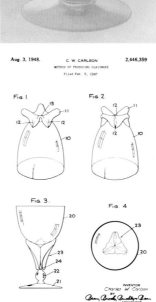

Top left: Afton #17537. Designed in 1952 by Edward J. Wormley. **$15-25**.

Top center: Aureole #17395, gold trim; Valencia #17361, gold trim. **$15-25** each.

Bottom left: Cellini #17423: Goblet, Champagne, Ice Tea, Cocktail, Claret, Sweet Wine. **$40-$50** each.

February 5, 1947, patent for the #17423 Cellini stemline, designed by Charles W. Carlson.

Crystal Cellini Goblet, very limited production, undocumented line number. **$45-65**.

Colonade #17601, bubble stem, gold trim. (Known as Lynndale with platinum trim.) **$15-25**.

Dawn #17690, platinum trim. **$15-25**.

Ducal #17674, gold trim. (Known as Classic with platinum trim.) **$15-25**.

Evening Mist #17688; Golden Spring #17688, gold trim. Evening Mist was produced on Smoke blanks. **$15-25** each.

Forever #17693, platinum trim. (Known as Betrothed with gold trim.) **$15-25**.

Golconda #17665, gold trim. (Known as Cara Mia with platinum trim.) **$15-25**.

Golden Spring #17688. **$15-25**.

Jefferson #17594, bubble stem. This same blank was earlier known as Mahal. It was renamed Jefferson under the ownership of Towle. **$15-25**.

June #17675, bubble stem, platinum trim. **$15-25**.

Leona #17670, gold trim. (Known as Sean with platinum trim.) **$15-25**.

109

Lovesong #17693. **$15-25**.

Lynndale #17601, platinum trim. (Known as Colonade with gold trim.) **$15-25**.

Majesty #17507, gold or platinum trim: Goblet, Wine, Champagne/Sherbet, Ice Tea. **$15-25** each.

Midas #17638, gold trim. (Known as Fairfax with platinum trim.) **$15-25**.

Ming Modern #17514, designed in 1951 by Edward J. Wormley. Ming Modern was available in six sizes: goblet, sherbet, claret, cocktail, ice tea, and oyster cocktail. **$15-25**.

Miramar #17501, platinum trim. **$15-25**.

Poise #17673, platinum trim. **$15-25**.

Rhapsody #17726, gold or platinum trim: Goblet, Wine, Champagne/Sherbet, Ice Tea. **$15-25** each.

Richmond #17538. The 17538 stemline was designed by Edward J. Wormley in 1952. **$15-25**.

Romance #17688, platinum trim. **$15-25**.

Tuscanny #17539, bubble stem. The #17539 stemline was designed in 1952 by Edward J. Wormley. Retail price was $30.00 per dozen. **$15-25**.

Sarita #17576, platinum trim. **$15-25**.

Sean #17670, platinum trim. (Known as Leona with gold trim.) **$15-25**.

Trillium
Crystal #17418: Ice Tea, **$15-25**; Wine, **$15-25**; Goblet, **$20-30**; Cordial, **$35-45**.

111

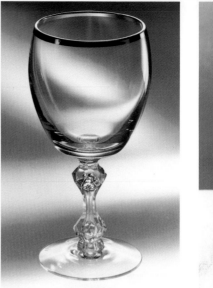

Westchester
Crystal #17679: Ice Tea, $40-$50; Wine, $45-55; Goblet, $45-55; Cocktail, $40-$50; Champagne, $40-$50; Flute Champagne, $50-60; Cordial, $70-80; #453, 9 oz. Old Fashion, $40-$50, bubble stem; all with Minton gold band.

Top left: Wind Song #17679, platinum trim. **$20-30**.

Top right: Tiffin Glass Goblet, undocumented stemline number. **$15-25**.

Bottom: #17604 line: Cocktail, Champagne, Claret, Rhine Wine, Whiskey Sour, Ale; all bubble stems. **$15-25** each.

Crystal Cocktail with tapered square stem, Paul Williams collection, attributed to Tiffin Glass. **$40-$50**.

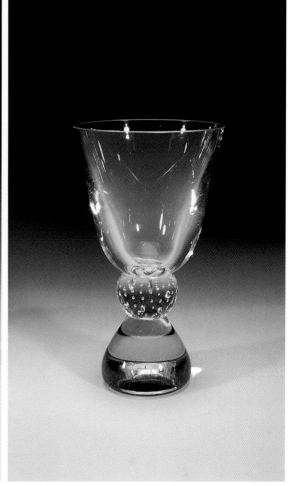

Crystal Chalice with paperweight base and controlled bubble connector, made by workers to be given to an incoming clergyman. **$150-175**.

Top left: Undocumented Tiffin Glass stems shown with Betsy Ross divided relish tray and comport. **$15-25** each.

Center left: Undocumented Tiffin Glass stems. **$15-25** each.

Bottom left: Undocumented Tiffin Glass stems. **$15-25** each.

Bottom right: Undocumented Tiffin Glass stem. **$15-25**.

Chapter 6
Hawkes Cuttings

HAWKES STEMWARE

Hawkes crystal . . . world-famous since 1880 . . . for those of discriminating taste.

In 1880, Thomas Gibbons Hawkes (1846-1913) founded the T. G. Hawkes Company in Corning, New York. The company was not a glass manufacturer, but purchased all of their ware for cutting from other glass companies, notably Corning Glass Works, Dorflinger, Steuben Glass Works, Libbey, and Val St. Lambert. In 1904, the United States Glass Company exhibited high quality Tiffin crystal blanks containing 33% lead content at the St. Louis World's Fair. Representatives from the Hawkes company were so impressed with the fine quality of the Tiffin blanks, that they purchased blanks from the Tiffin plant until the closing of the Hawkes factory in December 1962. The renowned Hawkes name was purchased in 1964 by the Tiffin Art Glass Company. The sale included all Hawkes patterns and the Hawkes trademark. The HAWKES name was sandblasted on the foot of all stemware, and a blue and white oval sticker was attached also. Tiffin continued the sale of Hawkes cuttings through 1973, with five of the original Hawkes patterns sold exclusively to Tiffany and Company. The Hawkes trademark is currently the property of Crystal Traditions of Tiffin, Ohio.

Aquila #6030. $50-60.

Left: Clarendon #6000. **$60-70.**

Center: Cornwall #7330. **$40-50.**

Right: Delft Diamond #7332. **$40-50.**

Left: Delft Diamond #7330. **$40-50.**

Right: Delft Diamond #6030. **$40-50.**

Left: Delft Diamond #6015. **$40-50.**

Center: Delft Diamond #6028. **$40-50.**

Right: Delft Diamond #7334. **$40-50.**

Left: Eardley #7334. **$40-50.**

Center: Eardley #7330. **$40-50.**

Right: Eardley #7332. **$40-50.**

EARDLEY 7240

7227 EARDLEY

LAURAL 2201

Left: Eardley #7240. **$40-50.**

Center: Eardley #7227. **$40-50.**

Right: Laural #2201. **$40-50.**

MALLORY 7332

MALLORY 7334

MANOR 7240

Left: Mallory #7332. **$40-50.**

Center: Mallory #7334. **$40-50.**

Right: Manor #7240. **$50-60.**

Left: Marcella #2201. **$50-60.**

Center: Royal #7334. **$40-50.**

Right: Strawberry Diamond and Fan #7332. **$50-60.**

MARCELLA 2201

ROYAL 7334

STRAWBERRY DIAMOND AND FAN 7332

Left: Strawberry Diamond and Fan #7240. **$50-60.**

Center: Strawberry Diamond and Fan #7227. **$50-60.**

Right: Strawberry Diamond and Fan #6028. **$50-60.**

STRAWBERRY DIAMOND 7227

Left: Strawberry Diamond and Fan #7334. **$50-60**.

Center: Tally Ho #7330. **$40-50**.

Right: Tally Ho #7332 **$40-50**.

Left: Tally Ho #7334 **$40-50**.

Right: Vernay #7334. **$40-50**.

Astor
Crystal: #7240 Goblet; #7227 Goblet; #7240 Goblet. **$50-75** each.

Top: Detail of Astor engraving.

Bottom: Detail of Hawkes paper label.

The Hawkes line recognized throughout the world by the connoisseurs of fine crystal as the Hallmark of perfection is being further enriched by the Tiffin artists.

7334 HEATHER
Hand-cut crystal diamonds highlight this superb interpretation of traditional design.

17594 HERMITAGE
Finely detailed cuttings blended with a classic shape . . .so precious to those of discriminating taste.

17683 RICHELIEU
Hand cuttings of grey and polished cuttings reflect the gracefulness and charm of refined dignity.

7240 MADISON
A pattern rich with history in the timeless tradition of cherished heirlooms.

17442 KILKENNY (left)
Poetry in crystal . . . magnificent in its blending of elegance and design to create an overall look of perfection.

17623 CONNEMARA
Perfection beautifully expressed by skilled artisans . . . for the most impressive decor.

17683 TULLAROAN (left)
The classic deft styling echoes the flawless beauty of opulent living.

17683 LA SCALA, GOLD
An exquisite lace cutting and a golden jeweled tiara united to create a pattern of rare artistry.

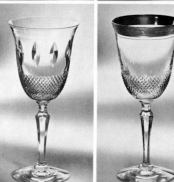

Top & bottom right: Hawkes by Tiffin
These eight designs were introduced in 1968 as Hawkes by Tiffin. Prices retailed in the *$10-$20* range.

Chapter 7
Tiffin Tradition

In 1979, Tiffin introduced 13 new patterns as the Tiffin Tradition line. Six sizes of stemware were offered, and all were signed with a script Tiffin logo. The price range for these was $70-100 each. In addition to the 12 patterns illustrated in the brochure, the Afton etching was available on the #17724 stemline with a gold band.

The Tiffin Tradition

The epitome of prestige crystal. Surpassing the master glass makers of the old world. Each piece of Tiffin Tradition has been made according to the highest standards of materials, design and craftsmanship.

The Tiffin Tradition line encompasses the two most desirable shapes in the land. A flared shape with tall notched stem and a bucket shape on multi-faceted stem with square cut and polished base.

All patterns are available in a generous size water goblet, #1 wine for fine burgundies, #2 wine for delectable white wines, gracefully shaped flute champagne for all sparkling wines, smartly designed sherry glass for sherry, port and dessert wines and the delightfully delicate cordial for fine liqueurs. Many patterns also available in 12 oz. highball, 10½ oz. on-the-rocks, 13½" decanter and 8" centerpiece bowl.

A multitude of designs are offered including deep mitre cuts, gold encrustations, gold-filled etching and banding, exquisite hand-cut florals and an etched oriental motif fully platinum-filled and banded. All pieces are signed 'Tiffin.'

Shown here:
Dijon . . . flared shape; motif is combination geometric and floral cut and polished design; rim has floral etching with 7/16th inch heavy gold encrustation. Available in all sizes.

Gabriel — Harvest — Gold Medallion — Dijon — Brittany — Victorian

Westerly — Chesterton — Leyland — Christina — Imperial Forest — Alexandria

The Tiffin Tradition

Top row shown left to right:
Gabriel . . . . exquisite example of floral cutting on flared shape bowl; stem is notched. Harvest . . . combination polished floral cutting and gray cut pear, apple and plum design; gray cutting on base. Gold Medallion . . . late nineteenth century gold-filled etching with heavy gold band laurel wreath. Dijon . . . flared shape combination cut, etching and 24kt gold decoration. Brittany . . . geometric punties and polished blaze cuttings; notched stem. Victorian . . . figural plate etching inscribed on cut and polished punties; rim has delicate laurel wreath etching.

Bottom row shown left to right:
Westerly . . . bucket shape with square base; deep mitred blaze and fleur-de-lis design. Chesterton . . . polished spike and ring design; polished square base. Leyland . . . deep cut polished drawn spikes and ring design; bucket shape. Christina . . . intricate floral and mitre cutting on faceted stem and square base. Imperial Forest . . . heavy platinum Minton band with oriental-inspired platinum-filled etching. Alexandria . . . heavy gold-encrusted floral band with gold-filled Flanders poppy motif.

Chesterton #17725: Goblet and Cordial. **$15-25**; **$20-30**.

Christina #17725: Salad Plate, Medium Wine, Goblet. The stemware is signed "Tiffin" on the foot. **$15-25**; **$40-50**; **$40-50**.

Gabriel #17724: Goblet, **$60-70**; Flute Champagne, **$60-70**; Decanter, **$250-300**; Highball, **$35-45**; On the Rocks, **$35-45**; Centerpiece Bowl, **$125-150**.

Gold Medallion #17724, Laurel gold band:
Goblet and Sherry. **$75-100** each.

Harvest #17724: Goblet and Sherry.
$60-70 each.

Westerly #17725: Highball, **$10-20**; Decanter, **$100-125**; Flute Champagne, **$15-25**; Large
Wine, **$15-25**; On the Rocks, **$10-20**; Centerpiece Bowl, **$35-45**.

Bottom left: Leyland #17725: Flute Champagne and Goblet. **$20-30** each.

Bottom center: Victorian #17724, Laurel band: Flute Champagne and Goblet . **$30-40** each.

Dijon
Crystal #17724: #1 Wine, **$65-85**; Goblet, **$65-85**; Sherry, #2, **$65-85**; Wine, **$65-85**; Cordial, **$100-125**; Flute Champagne, **$65-85**; all with cut stem and Melrose gold band, 1979 Tiffin Tradition line.

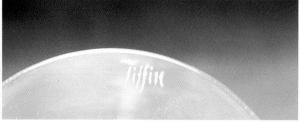

Top: Detail of Melrose gold band.

Bottom: Detail of acid stamped Tiffin logo on foot of stem. A 1967 Tiffin Glass Company catalog documents usage of the Tiffin "script" back stamp mark to identify stemlines in that publication. The "script" mark was also for identification of the stemlines included in the Tiffin Tradition line, introduced in 1979.

TIFFIN TRADITION CRYSTAL

PATTERN	Large Goblet	#1 Large Wine	#2 Medium Wine	Flute Champagne	Sherry	Cordial	Decanter 13½''	Centerpiece Bowl, 8½''	Highball	On-The-Rocks
Alexandria	$110.00	$110.00	$110.00	$110.00	$110.00	$110.00	---	---	---	---
Brittany	80.00	80.00	80.00	80.00	80.00	80.00	225.00	175.00	40.00	40.00
Chesterton	100.00	100.00	100.00	100.00	100.00	100.00	225.00	175.00	25.00	25.00
Christina	100.00	100.00	100.00	100.00	100.00	100.00	225.00	175.00	38.00	38.00
Dijon	85.00	85.00	85.00	85.00	85.00	85.00	225.00	175.00	55.00	55.00
Gabriel	80.00	80.00	80.00	80.00	80.00	80.00	225.00	175.00	38.00	38.00
Gold Medallion	70.00	70.00	70.00	70.00	70.00	70.00	---	---	---	---
Harvest	80.00	80.00	80.00	80.00	80.00	80.00	225.00	175.00	38.00	38.00
Imperial Forest	100.00	100.00	100.00	100.00	100.00	100.00	---	---	---	---
Leyland	90.00	90.00	90.00	90.00	90.00	90.00	225.00	175.00	32.00	32.00
Victorian	80.00	80.00	80.00	80.00	80.00	80.00	225.00	175.00	25.00	25.00
Westerly	100.00	100.00	100.00	100.00	100.00	100.00	225.00	175.00	28.00	28.00

1979 Tiffin Tradition price listing.

Harvest
Crystal #17724: Sherry, **$60-70**; #453, 10 ½ oz. Old Fashion, **$35-45**; 46 oz. Newton Decanter, undocumented line number, **$250-300**; #17724 Cordial, **$75-85**, 1979 Tiffin Tradition line.

Chapter 8
Matching Pattern Program

The Tiffin Art Glass Company introduced a matching pattern program, whereby once a year customers could replace breakage or add to original settings of over 750 retired Tiffin stemware shapes and patterns. In addition to cuttings and plate etchings, numerous blanks, and gold or platinum decorated stemware were offered.

A GREAT GOOD WILL BUILDER FOR YOU!

with the new and exclusive

matching pattern program

Now ... let your customers replace breakage or add to the Tiffin stemware they've cherished for years!

Over 750 Tiffin stemware shapes and patterns ... some going back 30 years and more ... are now on limited rerun. Don't let your customers be disappointed ... tell them the good news in your ads ... invite them to come in soon.

Get profitable repeat business ... work into wonderful new business

SINCE 1887

TIFFIN ART GLASS CORPORATION • TIFFIN, OHIO

TIFFIN'S
MATCHING PATTERN PROGRAM IS PART OF A GUARANTEED REPLACEMENT PROGRAM THAT IS UNIQUE WITH TIFFIN ART GLASS CORPORATION.

If you need more of these Matching Pattern Program Price Lists to cover your selling force, please send in your order at once. No charge, of course.

NOTE: See back cover for instructions in ordering and policies.

Here's an example of a beautiful Tiffin goblet, hand blown in 1940. One of many available in the Matching Pattern Program.

Line Number	Pattern	Stemware Each	Plate Each
17549	Dawn	7.25	8.00
17597	Daybreak	6.50	7.25
17652	Debbie	5.00	5.25
17601	Debut, Plat.	5.50	5.75
17453	Debutante	5.00	5.25
17524	Deby	6.50	7.00
17588	Decor	5.25	6.25
17591	Delphia	6.50	6.75
17358	Delys Optic	6.25	7.25
17358	Delys Plain	6.25	7.25
7565	Denise Pol.	6.25	6.75
7565	Denise, Grey	5.50	6.50
17613	Desert Flower	6.25	6.75
17666	Desert Song	5.00	5.25
17440	Devon	17.25	19.75
17644	Diamond, Plat.	3.75	5.25
17439	Diane	8.50	9.50
17501	Dimity, etched	4.50	5.00
17453	Dior	4.75	5.25
17301	Dior, Plat.	3.75	5.25
17625	Diplomat	8.00	8.50
17395	Dogwood	6.25	6.75
17418	Dolores	6.75	7.00
17627	Double Wedding, Plat.	6.50	8.25
17621	Druid	5.25	6.25
17594	Duchess	7.00	8.00
17643	Duet	5.00	5.50
D-8	Duncan Rose	8.75	9.25
17616	Dutchess of Devon	7.00	8.25
	E		
17624	Echo	6.75	7.25
17397	Ecstasy	7.25	8.00
17651	Ecstasy, Gold	3.75	5.25
17501	Eilene	7.00	7.00
17434	Elaine	5.00	5.25
17603	Electra	8.25	8.75
D-15	Elegance Regular	5.25	5.75
17507	Elinor	6.50	7.00
17660	Elite	4.75	5.00
17612	Elmhurst, Gold	8.25	8.75
17615	Elmhurst	5.50	6.25
17596	Elmwood, Gold Lx.	9.75	10.25
17664	Eloquence	4.50	4.50
17301	Embassy	4.25	5.25
17507	Embassy	6.50	6.50
17594	Emperor, Gold	8.25	8.25
17594	Empire, Gold	9.50	11.50
17489	Empress	9.25	10.25
17474	Enchanted	8.75	9.25
17594	Endearment	8.00	8.00
17648	Engagement, Gold	5.25	5.75
17651	Envoy	4.50	4.75
17660	Eos	4.50	4.75
17394	Erin	15.75	15.75
17581	Esplanade	7.25	8.00
17301	Essex	7.00	8.00
17536	Estelle	6.25	7.25
17507	Eternally Yours	6.50	6.75
17620	Ethereal	6.25	6.50
17616	Etude	5.00	5.50
17301	Even Song	8.00	9.00
17638	Everlasting	5.00	5.25
	F		
17647	Fair Lady, Gold	4.75	5.25
17625	Fairlawn	5.25	5.50
17574	Fairwind	5.00	5.50
17505	Fall Fantasy	6.75	7.25
17544	Falling Leaf	6.50	6.75
17431	Falmouth Sq. Ft.	20.25	19.75
17442	Falmouth Rd. Ft.	18.50	19.75
17492	Fantasy	8.25	8.75
17489	Fantasy, Old	8.25	8.75
17566	Fantasy	5.25	6.25
17524	Fascination	9.00	9.00
17492	Felecity	4.75	5.25
17492	Felicity, Old	4.75	5.25
17524	Fern	7.00	7.50
17644	Ferndale	4.75	5.00
17378	Ferndale	8.50	9.00
17597	Fernleaf	6.75	7.25
17524	Finesse	5.75	6.75
17627	First Lady	6.75	7.00
5111	First Love	5.00	5.50
7565	Flair	5.00	5.25
17603	Flair	6.25	6.25
17666	Flambeau	5.00	5.00
17670	Flame	4.75	5.00
17660	Flanders, Gold	5.75	6.50
17624	Flirtation	6.50	6.75
17566	Floral	6.50	6.75
17453	Florian	6.50	7.00
17492	Fluer De Lis	6.75	7.25
17630	Flurette	5.25	6.25
17669	Folia	4.50	4.75
17658	Fontaine, Plat.	4.75	6.25
17643	Fontana	5.25	5.25
17629	Forest Breeze	5.25	5.25
17661	Fortune, Plat	5.00	6.25
17546	Francis The First	7.25	8.00
17623	Frontence	9.75	10.25
17453	Fushia, etched	4.50	5.00
15083	Fuschia, etched	5.00	5.50
17624	Future Perfect, Plat	8.50	9.25
	G		
17643	Garland	5.25	5.75
5375	Garland	5.25	5.75
17654	Gayle, Plat.	4.75	6.25
17301	Gigi, Gold	3.75	5.25
17662	Glendora	5.00	5.25
17638	Golden Oak, Gold	5.50	8.00
17623	Gotham	10.75	11.00
17648	Grace, Plat.	5.00	6.25
17593	Granada	6.75	7.25
17640	Grandeur	5.50	5.75
17625	Grecian	6.25	6.50
17507	Greenbriar	7.00	7.00
17635	Greenbriar	5.25	5.75
17637	Green Briar, Gold	8.75	11.00
17657	Grosvenor	5.00	5.50
17621	Gypsy Rose	6.50	6.75
	H		
17589	Hacienda	6.50	7.00
17659	Hampton	16.25	16.25
17453	Harvest	6.50	7.00
17524	Harvest	6.50	7.00
17660	Hawthorne	5.25	5.50
17612	Heiress	6.25	6.75
17661	Heirloom	5.50	6.25
17578	Heritage	9.00	9.50
D-13	Heritage	6.75	7.00
17403	Hillcrest	8.25	8.75
17663	Hollins	5.00	5.25
17601	Honeysuckle	5.50	5.75
17551	Honeysuckle	4.75	5.25
17665	Horizon	4.75	5.00
17586	Hostess, Plat.	5.25	5.75
	I		
17358	Ibson	6.25	6.75
17666	Ice Rose	4.50	4.75
17665	Idyllic	4.50	4.75
17648	Inspiration	5.50	6.25
17618	Ione	5.25	6.25
17505	Ionic	5.25	5.75
17566	Iris	8.00	8.75
17546	Isis	5.25	5.75
17659	Ivanhoe	6.50	6.75
	J		
17651	Jamaica	4.50	5.00
17524	Jamestown	4.75	5.25
D-11	Janine	4.75	5.25
17597	Jasmine	5.25	5.25
17395	Jefferson	8.00	8.50
17395	Jefferson Flutes	7.25	7.25
17603	Jenifer	7.25	8.00
17664	Joan of Arc	5.25	6.50
17655	Joy Plat	5.25	6.25
17524	Jubilee, Gold	5.25	5.75
17598	Juliet	5.25	6.25
17524	June	5.75	6.50
17403	June Beau	8.50	8.75
17392	June Night	5.00	5.50
	K		
17492	Karen	6.50	7.00
17474	Karen	6.50	7.00
17347	Keats	6.75	7.25
17502	Kenilworth	7.25	10.25
40394	Kent	4.50	5.50
17301	Kent	6.50	6.75
17662	Kildare	5.25	5.25
15074	Killarney Green	4.75	5.75
17394	Killarney Green	4.75	5.75
17458	Killarney Green	4.75	5.75
17637	Killarney Green	5.25	5.75
17549	Kim	5.50	6.25
17594	King Lear	7.00	8.00
17594	King Richard	8.00	8.50
17392	Kingsley	7.00	8.25
17453	Kingsley	6.25	6.75
17578	Kohinoor	5.75	6.50
17624	Kristen	6.75	7.25
40548	Kristine	5.25	5.50
	L		
17525	Lace	5.25	6.25
17606	Ladonna	6.25	6.75
17524	Lady Carol	5.25	5.75
17524	Lady Fair	7.00	8.00
17507	Lady Hamilton	9.75	10.25
17507	Lady Louise	6.75	7.25
17651	Lady Love	4.50	5.50
17623	Lafayette	8.50	8.50
17630	Lahma, Plat	6.25	6.75
17536	Lairne	4.75	5.00
17551	Lamour	3.75	3.75
17646	Lanna	5.25	5.50
17566	Lark	5.00	5.50
17591	Larue	6.50	7.25
17625	Lasalle	6.50	6.75
17576	Lattice, Gold	6.50	7.00
17665	Laureate	4.75	5.00
17492	Laurel	8.25	8.75
17524	Laurel	5.50	6.50
17343	Laurel, Gold	7.25	8.75
17453	Laurel Wreath	5.25	5.75
17361	Laurel Wreath	6.25	6.75
17434	Laurent	6.75	7.25
17658	Lausanne	5.00	5.50
17524	Lavalier	5.25	5.75
17625	Leaves Golden	8.00	8.75
17434	Lehua	7.00	7.50
17439	Lehua	6.75	8.00
17667	Leilani	5.25	6.25
17440	Leland	13.25	13.25
17507	Lemar, Plat.	4.75	5.50
17454	Lenox Belvedere	7.25	8.75
17378	Lenox, Gold	9.50	11.00
17474	Lenox Rhodora	7.25	8.25
17612	Lenox Rose	6.75	7.00
17418	Lenox Wreath	5.50	6.50
17399	Lenox Wreath	5.50	6.50
17614	Lenox Wreath	6.50	6.50
17578	Lexington	6.50	7.00
17348	Liege	8.25	8.75
17394	Liege	8.75	9.25
7565	Lilt	6.25	6.75
DC-4	Lily of the Valley	7.00	8.25
D-4	Lily of the Valley	5.25	5.75
17378	Linda (Old)	7.25	8.00
17524	Linda	3.75	4.75
7565	Linear	5.25	5.50
17378	Londonberry	7.25	8.00
17665	Loraine	5.00	5.25
17394	Lord Nelson	10.25	10.25
17546	Lorelee	6.50	6.75
17524	Loretta	7.00	8.25
17670	Lori	5.00	5.25
17547	Lorna	6.25	6.75
17524	Louise	5.50	5.50
17358	Love Lace	5.00	5.50
17625	Lucerne	6.50	6.75
17624	Lynbrooke, Gold	6.50	6.75
17624	Lynnwood, Plat	5.00	6.25
17418	Lyric	6.50	7.25
17624	Lyric, Gold Lx.	8.75	10.25
	M		
17536	Madeira	6.75	7.25
17505	Madison	6.25	6.75
17566	Madrid	5.50	6.25
17625	Madrid	6.25	6.75
17546	Magnolia	5.00	5.50
17477	Magnolia, etched	4.50	5.00
17647	Majestic	4.75	5.25
17662	Majesty	5.00	5.00
17566	Malibu	5.25	6.25
17576	Manor	3.75	4.50
17566	Mara	5.25	5.50
17551	Marcia	6.25	6.75
17576	Marcia	5.25	5.75
D-13	Margaret Rose	7.00	7.00
17477	Marigold	7.00	8.00
17595	Marlene	7.00	7.50
17621	Marlene	6.25	6.50
17613	Marquis	6.25	6.50
17611	Marylyn	5.25	6.25
17630	May Dance	5.25	5.75
17525	Mayfair	6.75	8.00
17301	Mayflower, Grey	5.50	6.50
17301	Mayflower, Pol.	5.75	6.75
17651	Maytime	4.75	5.00
17601	Meadow Breeze	5.75	6.25
17591	Medallion	8.00	9.50
17596	Melbourne	6.75	7.00
17588	Melody	6.50	7.25
17657	Memory	4.50	4.75
15074	Melrose, Gold Green	12.25	12.25
17394	Melrose, Gold Green	12.25	12.25
17358	Melrose, Gold	6.75	8.25
17658	Merrileaf	5.00	5.25
17576	Mesa, Stain	5.75	6.25
17566	Mesa, Gold	6.75	7.00
17566	Mesa Grey	5.25	5.25
17566	Mesa Polish	5.25	5.25
17612	Meteor	6.25	6.75
17576	Metor	4.50	4.75
17601	Milady, Gold	8.50	9.00
17634	Milla	5.00	5.50
17637	Minerva	5.50	6.25
17477	Ming	7.00	8.00
17474	Ming	7.50	8.25
D-11	Ming Toy	5.25	5.25
17507	Minton, Gold	6.50	8.00
17505	Minton, Gold	6.75	8.75
17358	Minton, Gold	7.25	8.75
14196	Minton, Gold (14185)	6.75	8.75
15083	Minton, Gold	7.25	8.75
17394	Minton Green, Gold	11.50	11.50
15074	Minton Green, Gold	11.50	11.50
17603	Minuet	6.25	6.75
17492	Minuet	5.25	6.25
17361	Mirabelle	8.50	9.50
17658	Mirador	6.50	6.75
17659	Mirror Hvy.	7.00	7.25
17625	Mirror Pln.	8.00	8.25
17660	Mist	4.50	4.75
17614	Misty Leaf	6.75	7.25
17576	Mona Lisa, Gold	5.00	5.75
17574	Montclair, Plat. (Old)	5.00	6.25
17453	Montecarlo	5.00	5.50
17474	Montecarlo	5.50	5.50
17601	Monterey	5.75	6.25
17395	Monticello	5.00	5.50
17578	Monticello	5.75	6.75
17453	Moonglow, Plat.	4.75	5.50
17492	Moonlight	5.50	6.25
17624	Morning Star	6.50	7.25
17453	Moss Rose	8.50	8.50
17442	Mount Batten, Rd. Ft.	17.25	19.50
17431	Mount Batten, Sq. Ft.	19.50	19.50
17591	Mt. Vernon	5.00	5.50
17670	Musette	5.00	5.25
17667	Mussette	4.75	5.25
17651	My Sin, Plat.	3.75	5.25
17397	Mystic	9.50	13.25
17378	Mystic	9.50	13.25
	N		
17576	Nancy	5.00	5.25
17673	Nanette	4.50	4.75
17591	Natchez	5.50	6.75
17651	Newport	4.75	5.25
17547	Newport	6.25	7.25
17524	Nina	3.75	4.50
17453	Nobility	7.00	8.00
17659	Nobility	8.00	8.00
17667	Nocturne, Gold	5.00	6.75
17507	North Star	6.75	8.00
17623	Notre Dame	10.75	11.00
17418	Nydia, Gold	6.25	6.75
	O		
17663	Oberlin	5.00	5.25
17553	Old Colonial	6.50	7.25
17477	Old Master	8.50	9.00
	P		
17603	Palm	6.25	6.75
17596	Palm	5.00	5.25
17596	Palmento	5.25	6.50
17477	Pamela	5.25	5.75
17524	Pandora	8.00	9.00
17634	Paradise	5.00	5.50
17670	Parisienne	4.75	5.00
17616	Park Lane	6.75	7.25
17501	Patricia	6.50	7.00
17660	Patricia, Gold	5.00	5.25
17524	Pavlova	5.75	6.50
17477	Peach Tree	7.00	8.00
17640	Peach Tree	4.75	5.25
17474	Lx. Peach Tree	8.00	8.50
17665	Periwinkle	4.50	4.75
17666	Perpetua	5.25	5.25
17358	Persian Pheasant	5.00	5.50
17392	Persian Pheasant	5.00	5.50
17501	Petit Point, Pol.	6.25	6.50
17501	Petit Point, Gray	5.75	5.75
D-11	Petite	5.00	6.25
17595	Petite	6.75	6.75
17603	Petite	6.75	6.75
17665	Petite Fluer	5.00	5.25
17453	Phyllis	8.00	8.75
17524	Picardy	4.75	5.25
17660	Picardy	4.75	5.25
17574	Picardy	5.25	6.25
17525	Pickfair	6.75	7.25
17574	Lx. Pine	6.75	7.25
17547	Pine Cone	9.75	10.25
17418	Pine Cone	9.75	10.25
17546	Pinehurst	6.25	6.50
17552	Pinehurst	6.25	6.50
17477	Pine Tree	8.75	9.00
17474	Pine Tree	9.75	10.25
17492	Pine Tree	9.75	10.25
D-13	Pine Tree	6.25	6.75
17507	Pinewood	5.25	5.75
17507	Pirouette	5.00	5.50
17568	Plymouth	6.75	6.75
17614	Poinsetta	6.50	7.25
17673	Poise, Plat.	3.75	5.25
17601	Polka	5.25	5.75
17613	Pompeii, Plat.	4.50	5.00
17442	Precedent Rd. Ft.	16.75	19.75
17492	Prelude	6.50	6.75
17442	Prestige Rd. Ft.	29.25	29.25
17431	Prestige Sq. Ft.	32.25	29.25
17665	Priam	4.75	5.00
17477	Prince Charming	9.00	10.25
17594	Princess Eugenia	8.50	8.75
17603	Princess Issena	6.75	7.25
17597	Princess, Plat.	6.75	7.25
17566	Princess Rose, Plat.	6.75	8.25
17566	Princess Rose	5.25	6.75
17507	Princess Rose	6.25	6.50
17597	Princess	6.50	7.25
17492	Princess	8.75	9.25
17361	Priscilla	6.25	6.75
17431	Pristine, Sq. Ft.	20.75	17.25
17442	Pristine, Rd. Ft.	17.25	17.25
17651	Promise	4.50	5.50
17434	Propinquity (Rosalie)	7.25	8.75
17361	Propinquity	7.25	8.75
17618	Prudence	6.25	6.75
17361	Puritan, Grey	7.00	7.50

Line Number	Pattern	Stemware Each	Plate Each
Q			
17349	Queen Ann	5.25	5.75
5375	Queen Lace	5.00	5.50
R			
17616	Radcliff	6.75	6.75
D-11	Radiance	5.25	6.75
17477	Rain (Crystal)	4.50	5.25
17551	Rain (Crystal)	4.50	5.25
17477	Rain (Pink)	4.50	5.25
17657	Raindrop	4.50	4.75
14196	Rambler Rose, Gold	6.75	8.75
17594	Rameses	9.00	9.00
17524	Random	5.25	5.75
17591	Rappidan	6.75	6.75
17651	Rapture, Plat.	3.75	5.25
17551	Ravel	4.75	5.25
17655	Reflection	6.25	6.75
17474	Reflexicone	7.25	8.00
D-13	Regency	6.75	7.25
17394	Regent	14.00	14.00
17300	Regent, Gold	7.00	7.25
17601	Regina	6.25	6.50
17603	Resplendent	7.00	7.25
17612	Revelation	6.25	6.75
17648	Reverie	5.00	5.50
D-3	Reverie	4.50	6.25
17524	Reverie	6.50	7.00
17670	Rhapsody	4.75	5.00
D-15	Rhythm	6.25	8.25
17596	Rialto	5.50	5.75
17625	Richmond	6.75	7.25
17492	Ridgewood	5.25	6.25
17547	Ripple	5.25	6.25
17507	Rita	7.00	8.00
17667	Riviera, Gold	4.75	6.25
17502	Rockwood	5.25	5.75
17524	Romance	3.75	4.50
17644	Romance	4.75	5.50
17453	Romance	4.75	5.25
17593	Romantique	6.75	7.00
17467	Rondo	5.00	5.25
17434	Rosalie (Propinquity)	7.25	8.75
17492	Rosalind	11.00	12.75
17477	Rose, etched	4.50	5.00
17474	Rose, etched	5.00	5.50
17492	Rose Leaf	9.50	9.50
17501	Rose Marie, etched	4.50	5.00
17507	Rose of Picardy, etched	4.50	5.00
17603	Rose of Sharon	6.50	7.00
17601	Roselyn	5.75	5.75
17660	Rosemont	4.50	4.50
17394	Roslyn	6.75	7.00
17654	Royal Coronet	5.50	6.50
17454	Royal Fern	5.25	6.50
17655	Royal Tiara	6.50	6.75
17453	Royal Wreath	4.75	5.25
17503	Royal York	6.25	6.75
17621	Rubicon, Plat.	5.25	7.25
17474	Rutledge	7.50	8.25
17474	Lx. Rutledge	8.75	9.50
17477	Rutledge	5.75	6.50
17477	Lx. Rutledge	8.00	8.50
S			
17492	Saba, Plat	7.25	8.00
17591	Sabina	6.25	6.75
17652	Sakarra	6.50	6.75
17640	Salem	5.00	5.25
17549	Salisbury	5.00	5.50

Line Number	Pattern	Stemware Each	Plate Each
17536	Sandra	6.50	6.75
17625	Sandra	6.75	7.25
17651	Sandra, Gold	3.75	5.25
17492	Santa Anita	5.50	6.50
17403	Saturn, Gold	6.25	6.75
17614	Saxony	6.25	6.50
17624	Scroll, Gold	6.75	7.25
17651	Sentiment	3.75	4.75
17598	Sequence	6.25	6.50
17607	Sequin	6.25	6.75
17492	Serenity	7.25	8.00
17638	Seventeen	5.25	5.50
17477	Seville	6.25	6.50
17547	Shalimar	5.25	5.75
17500	Shannon	5.50	6.75
17574	Shasta	6.25	6.75
17502	Sheffield	5.50	6.25
17546	Shelton	8.25	8.50
17576	Sherwood	4.50	5.00
D-3	Sherwood	4.75	5.75
17637	Shining Star	5.50	6.25
17608	Siam	5.25	6.25
17644	Siesta	4.75	5.25
17474	Silhouette	5.50	6.25
17492	Silverdale, Plat.	7.25	8.75
17601	Silverdale, Plat.	6.50	8.00
17596	Silverleaf, Plat.	5.50	6.50
17667	Silverne, Plat.	6.25	7.25
17618	Silver Spray, Plat.	6.50	6.75
17601	Silver Spray, Plat.	5.50	5.75
17601	Silver Star, Plat.	5.75	6.75
17614	Silverstone, Plat.	6.50	7.25
D-16	Silver Symphony, Plat.	4.50	5.00
17546	Silver Wheat	6.75	8.00
17536	Silver Wheat	6.75	8.00
17540	Silver Wheat	6.75	8.00
17453	Silver Wheat	5.75	6.75
17524	Silver Wheat	5.75	6.75
D-3	Silver Wheat	4.50	5.25
17477	Silver Wreath, Plat.	6.25	7.00
17665	Sincerity	4.25	4.50
17547	Sir Winston	6.25	6.75
17660	Skylark	3.75	4.50
17507	Skylark	4.75	5.00
17551	Skylark (New)	4.75	5.00
17643	Snowberry	5.00	5.50
17601	Snow Tulip	5.75	6.25
17612	Solitaire, Gold	6.75	7.25
17612	Solitaire, Plat.	5.25	5.75
17566	Sonnet	5.00	5.50
17551	Sophistication	3.75	4.75
17658	Sorrento	7.25	8.50
17546	Southern Star	8.00	8.75
17586	South Wind	6.25	6.75
17633	Spartan	5.25	6.50
D-15	Splendor	6.75	7.00
17505	Spray	6.75	8.00
17576	Spring	5.50	5.75
D-5	Spring Beauty	6.25	7.25
17651	Spring Blossom	4.75	5.00
17501	Spring Flower	5.00	5.50
7565	Spring Flower	6.50	7.25
17576	Spring Glory	4.75	5.00
17624	Spring Love	6.50	7.00
17576	Spring Rhythm	4.75	5.00
17551	Spring Shower	4.50	4.75
17670	Spring Song	4.50	4.75
17490	Spring Song	6.75	8.00
17665	Springtide	4.50	4.75
17434	Springtime, etched	5.00	5.50
17453	Springtime, etched	4.50	5.00
17650	Sprite	5.25	6.25

Line Number	Pattern	Stemware Each	Plates Each
17553	Squire	6.25	6.50
17658	Staccato, Gold	5.00	6.75
17480	Staffordshire	7.25	8.00
17574	Starbright	5.00	5.00
17640	Stardust	4.75	5.25
17551	Stardust	5.50	6.50
17601	Starfire	5.00	5.50
17634	Starfire	6.75	6.75
D-8	Starlight	8.25	8.25
17542	Starlight	6.75	8.25
17536	Starlight	6.75	8.25
17403	Starlight	6.75	8.25
17536	Starlight	6.75	8.25
17442	Stem Rd. Ft.	11.50	14.00
17431	Stem Sq. Ft.	17.25	14.00
17608	Stoddard	6.75	7.25
17616	St. Charles	6.75	7.25
17524	Strand	7.00	8.00
17651	Summertime	4.50	5.25
17576	Summer Wheat, Stain	6.50	6.50
17566	Summer Wheat, Plat.	7.25	7.25
17566	Sunburst	6.75	7.25
17644	Sunflower, Gold	5.50	5.50
17477	Sunnyvale, Plat.	6.25	7.00
17617	Sunrise	6.50	6.75
17395	Surrey	7.25	9.50
17525	Sussex	6.75	8.00
17652	Suzanne, Plat.	5.25	6.25
17614	Swirl	6.50	6.75
17586	Sylphide	5.25	5.75
17621	Sylvan	5.25	5.25
17669	Sylvia, Plat.	5.50	5.75
17453	Sylvia	5.75	7.50
17666	Symphony, Plat.	4.50	5.25
T			
17399	Talisman, Gold	8.25	8.75
17403	Talisman, Gold	8.25	8.75
17548	Tara	6.25	6.75
17610	Tasso	5.25	6.25
17453	Tea Rose, etched	4.50	5.00
17636	Tempo	6.25	6.50
17650	Tenderly	5.00	5.25
17418	Teresa	7.00	8.25
17394	Terrance	6.25	6.75
17636	Thea	6.25	6.50
17546	Theda	6.50	7.25
17658	Theme	4.75	5.25
17453	Thistle	6.75	8.25
17489	Tiara	8.75	9.50
17395	Tiffin Optic	5.00	—
17441	Tiffin Rose, etched	5.00	5.50
17603	Tiger Lily	5.50	6.25
17397	Tiger Lily, Old	9.25	9.25
17551	Tina (Old)	5.00	5.75
17566	Tina	4.75	5.25
17625	Tipperay	6.75	6.75
17609	Tivoli	6.25	6.75
17625	Toulouse	7.25	8.00
17442	Trafalgar, Rd. Ft.	20.25	20.25
17431	Trafalgar, Sq. Ft.	33.00	20.25
17612	Traymore	7.00	8.00
17608	Trellis	6.75	7.25
17476	Trellis, Old	6.25	6.75
17603	Trenton	7.00	7.25
17614	Triad	6.50	6.75
17566	Trianon	4.75	5.25
17615	Trieste, Plat	5.25	5.75
7565	Trina	4.75	5.00
17492	Trinidad, Plat.	7.00	8.25
17660	Tristan	4.50	4.75
5115	Tristan	11.50	11.50

Line Number	Pattern	Stemware Each	Plates Each
17625	Troth	6.75	6.75
17395	Trousseau	8.75	9.25
17378	True Love	8.75	10.25
17644	True Love, Gold	4.75	5.50
17524	Tryst	4.75	4.75
17666	Tudor	5.75	5.75
17624	Tuxedo, Gold	6.50	6.75
17603	Tuxedo, Gold	6.50	7.00
17574	Twirl	6.50	6.75
17651	Twinkle	5.00	5.00
17651	Twinkle, Plat.	5.00	5.25
V			
17361	Valencia, Gold	6.25	6.50
17457	Vanity Grey	6.75	8.25
17655	Ventura	5.50	6.50
17546	Venus	7.00	7.50
17525	Verona	6.25	6.75
17669	Vespera	5.25	5.75
17627	Vestal	5.50	5.75
17623	Vestavia	11.00	11.00
17502	Victoria	7.25	8.25
17536	Vida Gray	4.50	5.25
17348	Viking	9.50	10.75
D-13	Vintage	5.25	6.25
D-3	Vintage	4.75	5.50

Line Number	Pattern	Stemware Each	Plates Each
17596	Vista	5.75	5.75
17524	Vivian	5.50	5.50
17658	Vivienne	6.50	6.50
17546	Vocari	5.25	5.75
17625	Vogue	6.50	6.75
W			
17301	Wallingford	6.25	6.75
17301	Wallingford Spikes	5.75	6.50
17595	Waltz of Spring	6.75	8.00
17442	Waterford, Rd. Ft.	17.25	17.25
17431	Waterford Sq. Ft.	26.50	17.25
17596	Waverly	6.25	6.50
17418	Wedding Day, Plat.	5.00	6.50
17501	Wedding Ring	5.25	6.25
17591	Wellington	5.50	6.25
17670	Westminister	5.00	5.25
17394	Westover	11.00	11.00
17574	Westwind	6.50	6.75
17500	Westwood	5.25	5.75
17546	Wheat, Golden	9.50	11.00
17542	Wheat, Golden	9.50	11.00
17540	Wheat, Golden	9.50	11.00
17551	Wheat, Golden	6.75	9.00
17536	Wheat, Golden	9.50	11.00
17648	Whisper	4.75	5.25
17671	Whitehouse	9.50	9.50
17595	Wild Flower	6.50	7.00

Line Number	Pattern	Stemware Each	Plates Each
17667	Wild Rose	5.00	5.25
D-3	Wild Rose	6.50	8.00
17395	Williamsburg	5.25	5.75
17489	Willow	5.50	7.00
17665	Windfall	4.50	4.75
17395	Winding Wreath	6.75	8.00
17638	Windsor	5.00	5.75
17348	Windsor	7.00	8.75
17658	Windswept	5.50	6.25
17632	Winston	5.50	6.50
D-3	Winston	5.00	5.75
17646	Winter Eve	4.75	5.00
17624	Wishing Star	6.50	6.75
17546	Wisp	6.75	7.25
17613	Wistaria, Cut	6.25	6.50
17652	Woodlawn	5.25	5.75
17650	Woodlore	5.00	5.25
17347	Woodstock	5.25	6.25
17301	Woodstock	4.75	5.25
17637	Worchester	5.25	6.75
17378	Wreath	6.25	6.75
17348	Wreath	6.75	7.25
17477	Wreath, Gold	6.75	9.00
17651	Wyndcrest	3.75	4.75
Z			
17566	Zenith, Gold	8.00	8.25

STEMWARE BLANKS

The following section contains goblet illustrations of "C" Pattern Tiffin blanks which comprise the Tiffin Matching Pattern Program. Each is identified by a line number which should be plainly indicated on your order. This section will assist you in selecting the correct blank on which your customer's pattern is to be made. Blanks for stemware other than goblets will conform to the illustrations shown. Assure your customer that any piece (iced tea, sherbet, claret, etc.) can be duplicated if blank selection is properly made. Have customer particularly note general bowl contour, stem design and configuration, and style of pedestal.

Note: Illustrations with an asterisk (*) denote shape has bubble stem.

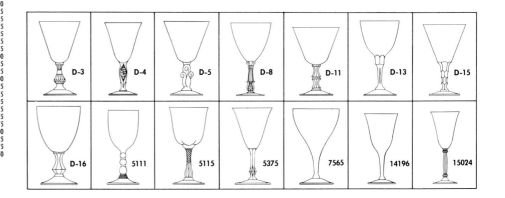

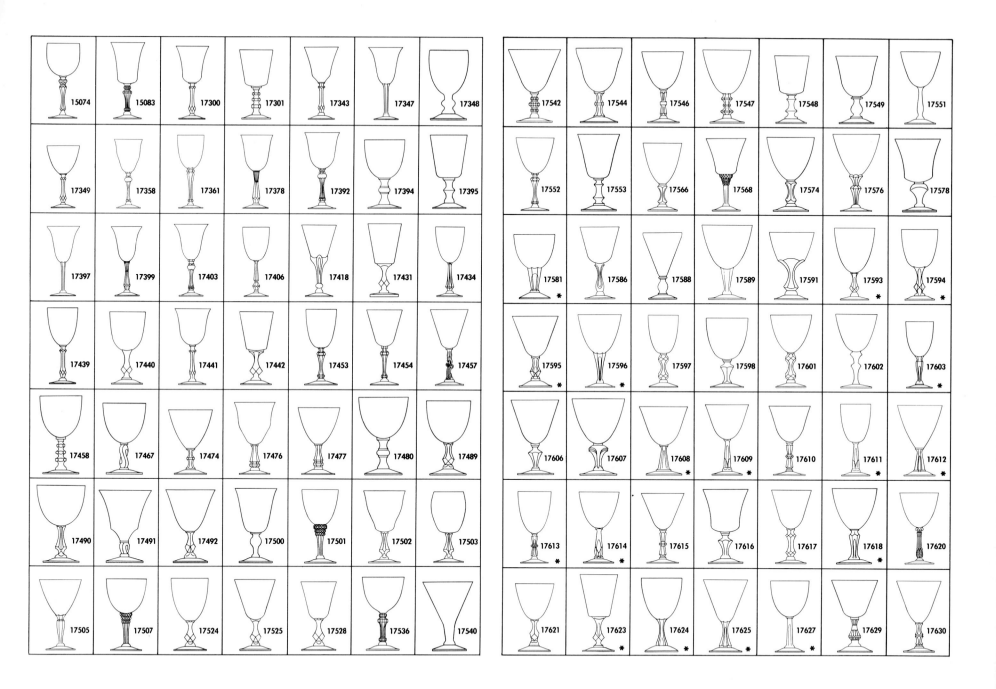

15074 · 15083 · 17300 · 17301 · 17343 · 17347 · 17348
17349 · 17358 · 17361 · 17378 · 17392 · 17394 · 17395
17397 · 17399 · 17403 · 17406 · 17418 · 17431 · 17434
17439 · 17440 · 17441 · 17442 · 17453 · 17454 · 17457
17458 · 17467 · 17474 · 17476 · 17477 · 17480 · 17489
17490 · 17491 · 17492 · 17500 · 17501 · 17502 · 17503
17505 · 17507 · 17524 · 17525 · 17528 · 17536 · 17540

17542 · 17544 · 17546 · 17547 · 17548 · 17549 · 17551
17552 · 17553 · 17566 · 17568 · 17574 · 17576 · 17578
17581 · 17586 · 17588 · 17589 · 17591 · 17593 · 17594
17595 · 17596 · 17597 · 17598 · 17601 · 17602 · 17603
17606 · 17607 · 17608 · 17609 · 17610 · 17611 · 17612
17613 · 17614 · 17615 · 17616 · 17617 · 17618 · 17620
17621 · 17623 · 17624 · 17625 · 17627 · 17629 · 17630

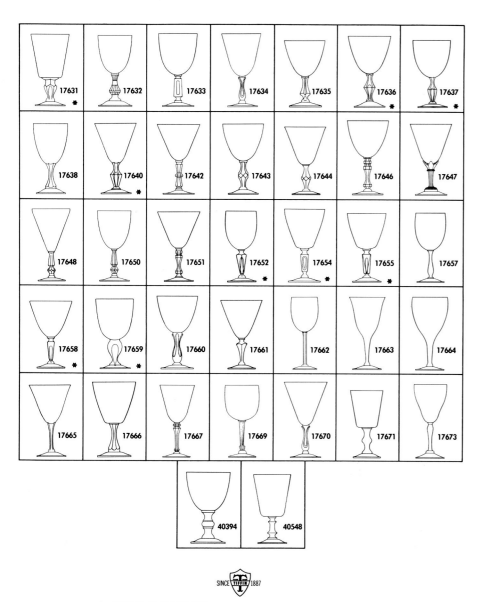

17631 * | 17632 | 17633 | 17634 | 17635 | 17636 * | 17637 *
17638 | 17640 * | 17642 | 17643 | 17644 | 17646 | 17647
17648 | 17650 | 17651 | 17652 * | 17654 * | 17655 * | 17657
17658 * | 17659 * | 17660 | 17661 | 17662 | 17663 | 17664
17665 | 17666 | 17667 | 17669 | 17670 | 17671 | 17673

40394 | 40548

SINCE **TIFFIN** 1887

TIFFIN IS FOREVER—*Patterns Produced Since 1887 Available Today*

Tiffin matching pattern program...

how to order

The preceding pages carry an alphabetical listing of all Tiffin non-current patterns available. Following the pattern listings are illustrations of goblet blanks to enable your customer to select the correct shape of her stemware.

To safeguard against inaccurate pattern designation, a tissue rubbing of the cutting must accompany the order.

how to take a tissue rubbing

This is a fast and very simple procedure.

Merely overlay the pattern with a piece of tissue paper and go back and forth over the tissue surface with the flat edge of a soft lead pencil. This will bring out the pattern in a fashion distinct enough for positive identification of the pattern by the factory.

policy

Cut-off date for the acceptance of orders for inactive patterns is November 1st. The month of December will be devoted to the manufacture and shipment of all orders placed under the matching pattern program.

Craftsmanship in Glass   SINCE 1887

TIFFIN ART GLASS CORPORATION • TIFFIN, OHIO

"What is Tiffin? TIFFIN is design excellence with unparalleled perfection and elegance that has been the goal and achievement of 100 years of experience in the manufacture of fine handmade stemware and table accessories."

Chapter 9
Masterpiece Collection

The Masterpiece Collection, which was introduced in 1979, featured a line of plain Crystal tableware accessories. The Sherwood candlestick was originally produced circa 1961 in the colors of Golden Banana, Plum, Copen Blue, and Crystal. The Newton decanter was also a part of the 1979 Tiffin Tradition line and can be found with the Gabriel, Westerly, Harvest, Victorian, Brittany, Chesterton, Christina, Dijon, and Leyland patterns. The Empress bud vase was produced in black, blue, and a pale pink color.

The Tiffin Masterpiece Collection
of hand blown lead crystal gifts.

Brilliant, handmade, gleaming, luxurious lead crystal pieces of substantial weight.

Magnificently finished, each piece is individually boxed and has the Tiffin signature delicately etched into the crystal for generations to cherish.

Notice the simplicity of design, the clarity and blue-white color of the crystal. Contemporary in appeal yet traditional in design, the Masterpiece Collection is a tribute to the meticulous talents of Tiffin's master craftsmen. At home in any decor, the initial eleven piece collection will be received as a lasting gift of beauty and practicality.

Shown: Beacon Hill Bowl, Newton Decanter, Tiffin Trumpet Vase, Sherwood Candlestick and Porter Decanter/Carafe.

The Tiffin Masterpiece Collection

Ophelia Bud Vase
This slender teardrop-shaped vase is a superb vehicle to display the single perfect stem. 8¼" tall.

Beacon Hill Bowl
An authentic replica of the famous Paul Revere design, this bowl performs well as centerpiece or server. 8¼" diameter.

Empress Bud Vase
Reminiscent of the classic oriental jar, a lovely way to show your favorite poseys. 6¼" tall.

Justine Carafe
An expression of beauty for bar, table or floral arrangements. 9¾" tall—holds 38 oz.

Sherwood Candlesticks
Dignified simplicity yet definitely at home in any period. Baluster stem encases trapped teardrop. 5" tall.

Countess Bud Vase
The bulbous shape adequately supplies long life to a single rose. 6" tall.

Brookfield Cruets
Beautiful and practical, these oil & vinegar cruets harmonize with any table setting or buffet. 7½" tall.

Newton Decanter
A dramatic accent to dining table or bar, this stunning decanter 13½" tall comfortably holds 46 oz. of liquid.

Tiffin Trumpet Vase
Classic in design, our 8½" trumpet is ideal for taller stemmed flowers. Appealing as an art form in shimmering crystal.

Porter Decanter/Carafe
Perfect for whiskeys, brandies and the like, this beauty also doubles as a wine or water carafe. 10" tall, 40 oz.

Van Cleve Bowl
Classically styled, to be used for salads, fruits or floral arrangements. Handsome as a decorative accessory. 8" diameter.

1979 pamphlet showing some of the items available in the Masterpiece Collection.

Chapter 10
Compotes

Compotes were an important part of Tiffin's tableware accessories until the mid 1960s. All of the compotes included in this chapter are blown ware, produced from the late 1940s through 1965. The #5501 compotes were made in Crystal only, and were decorated to match stemware patterns.

Left: Compotes with cuttings to coordinate with stemware patterns.

Center: Compotes with cuttings to coordinate with stemware patterns.

COMPOTES BY
Tiffin

There is a lifetime of enjoyment in store for you with your selection of a handblown handcut compote fashioned by the Tiffin Glassmasters. Unique cuttings have been designed to complement any decor.

5501
Bristol

5501
Pristine

5501
Mirage

5501
Fordham

5501
Plain

5501
King Arthur

5501
Gold Palais Versailles

5501
Leland

5501
Resplendent

Top: Twilight #6447, 6" Compote, Tiffin Optic. **$125-150**.

Bottom: Killarney with Crystal trim #17394-5, 7". Compote. **$65-90**.

Killarney with Crystal trim: #17394-6, 4" h. Candlesticks, **$100-125** pair; #17394-6, 6 ¼" Compote, **$65-90**.

Tiffin Rose, Cobalt Blue with Crystal trim #6109, 7 ¼" Compotes, Diamond Optic, **$175-200** each; Crystal with Black trim #15037 Goblet, Wide Optic, **$35-45**; Plum #6109, 7 ¼" Compote, Diamond Optic, **$125-150**. The compotes date from the early 1960s and use the same stem as the goblet that dates from about 1930. The United States Glass Company was in financial straits in the early 1960s and used parts of old molds to save on costs.

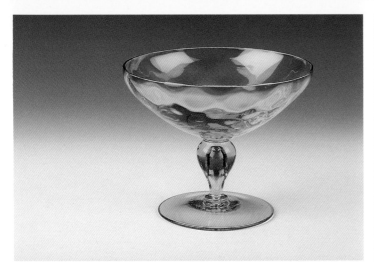

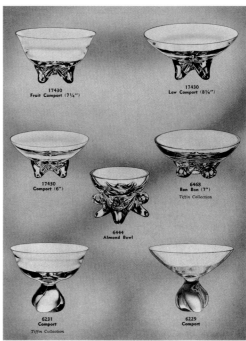

Top left: Golden Banana #6111, 5 ¼" Compote, Diamond Optic, 1961. **$125-150**.

Top center: #5442 Compote. **$35-45**.

Top right: #5501, #5503, #5500 Compotes; all bubble stems. **$35-45** each.

Bottom left: Citron Green #17423, 6" Compote, Tiffin Optic, Cellini line, c.1965. **$175-225**.

Bottom center & right: 1951 catalog page.

Chapter 11
Decanters

The majority of the Tiffin Modern decanters were produced around 1945 through 1955, predominantly in Crystal. A number of these decanters were decorated with cuttings or sand carved designs. The blown stopper usually contained a bubble, and most were ground and polished. A numbering system was used to mark the stopper and decanter, assuring a proper match. The stopper was numbered on the bottom; a matching number was engraved on the lip or neck of the decanter.

Top left: Early 1940s *China, Glass and Lamps* advertisement by the United States Glass Company featuring the #577 decanter.

Bottom left: September 1941 *China, Glass and Lamps* advertisement by the United States Glass Company featuring the #577, #3700, and #5918 decanters.

Left: Crystal #32592 Cordial Decanter, undocumented cutting. **$125-150**.

Center: Crystal #3700 Decanter, undocumented cutting and #5443 Decanter; both bubble stoppers. **$75-100** each.

Right: Crystal Wine Decanter, unknown line number, c.1954. **$100-125**.

Crystal #13624 Decanter, Dog engraving, Tiffin Optic.
$125-150.

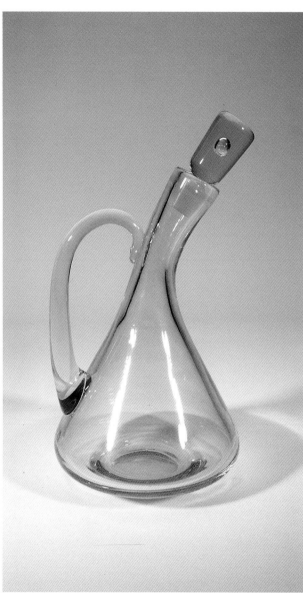

Twilight #3 Wine Bottle with "Teardrop" stopper, applied
handle. There is also a smaller size, #2 Cordial bottle.
Made for the January 3, 1952, Pittsburgh Glass Trade
Show. **$300-350**.

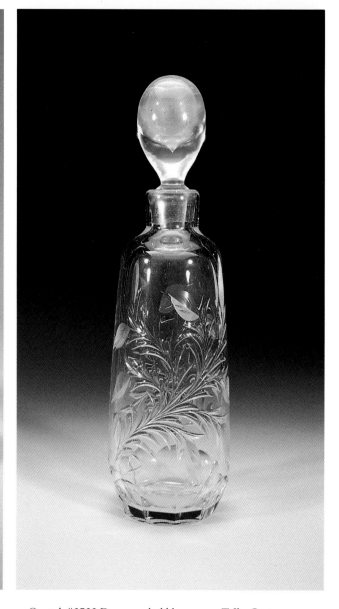

Crystal #3700 Decanter, bubble stopper, Tiffin Optic,
undocumented cutting. **$125-150**.

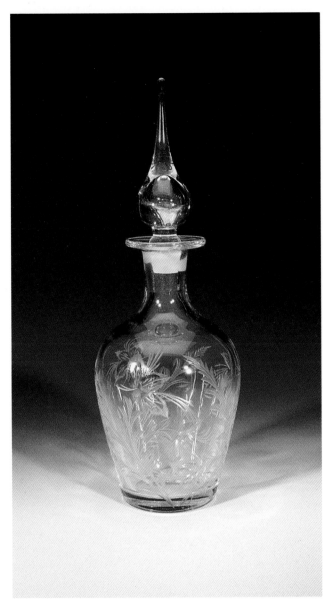

Crystal #13624 Decanter, bubble stopper, undocumented cutting. **$100-125**.

Crystal #5443 Decanter, bubble stopper, undocumented engraving. **$125-150**.

Crystal #5413, 8 ¾" h. Cocktail Shaker, Tiffin Optic. **$75-100**.

Citron Green Decanter, bubble stopper, undocumented line number, limited production, c.1965. **$200-250**.

Crystal #5405 Antique Whiskey Jug. Jug has four green ribbons on side and two green ribbons on neck, and feather shape handle. Stopper is 2 ¼" square and has large bubble in center. Made for the January 1954 Glass Trade Show and was available for $6.00, very limited production. **$200-250**.

Crystal #5402 Decanter with Rigaree, "Teardrop" stopper, 1954. **$150-200**.

Twilight #5402 Decanter with Rigaree trim, "Teardrop" stopper, 1954. **$300-350**.

Twilight #17501 Cordial; #5403 Decanter with Rigaree trim, "Teardrop" stopper, undocumented engraving by Fred Windstine. **$75-100; 300-350**.

Killarney with Crystal trim #17437 Cordial Decanter, and Oil Bottle, c.1950. **$150-175; $100-125**.

#5439 Decanter.
$65-80.

3700 DECANTER,
SWEDISH OPTIC
Capacity—24 oz.

577 SWEDISH TYPE
DECANTER
Flanged Neck   Heavy Base
Capacity—36 oz.

32592 CORDIAL
DECANTER
Swedish Optic
Capacity—12 oz.

5918 SQUARE
DECANTER
Pinched Sides
Capacity—20 oz.

5970 DECANTER,
SPIRAL OPTIC
Capacity—32 oz.

1940 Catalog page.

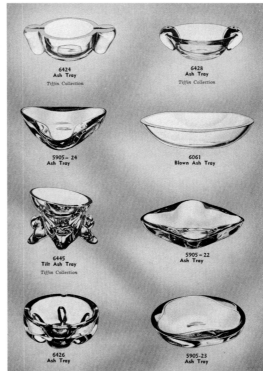

6424
Ash Tray
Tiffin Collection

6428
Ash Tray
Tiffin Collection

5905—24
Ash Tray

6061
Blown Ash Tray

6445
Tilt Ash Tray
Tiffin Collection

5905—22
Ash Tray

6426
Ash Tray

5905-23
Ash Tray

1940 Catalog page.

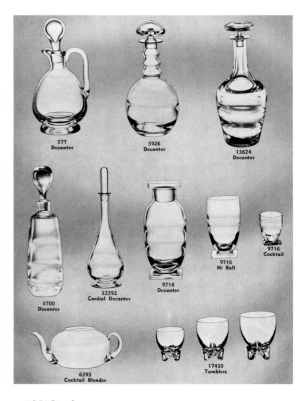

577
Decanter

5926
Decanter

13624
Decanter

3700
Decanter

32592
Cordial Decanter

9716
Decanter

9716
Hi Ball

9716
Cocktail

6393
Cocktail Blender

17430
Tumblers

1951 Catalog page.

140

Chapter 12
Jugs

Many different styles of Modern jugs were produced from 1940 to 1955. These blown containers are usually found in Crystal; however, examples can be found in Killarney, Wistaria, Twilight, Copen Blue, Smoke, and Black. The #5959 jug was sometimes decorated with Cherokee Rose, June Night, Fuchsia, or Springtime plate etchings.

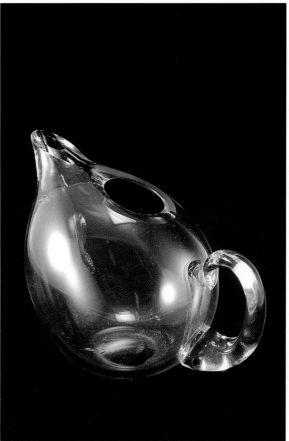

Top left: Crystal, Tiffin Optic: #2 Jug; #5961 Jug; both bubble stem, Tiffin Optic. **$85-110** each.

Bottom left: Crystal Jug, attributed to Tiffin. **$75-100**.

Top right: Crystal #1 Cocktail Blender, c. 1950. **$75-100**.

Bottom right: Copen Blue 9 ¼" h. and 11 ½" h. Jugs, probably non-production items. **$125-150** each.

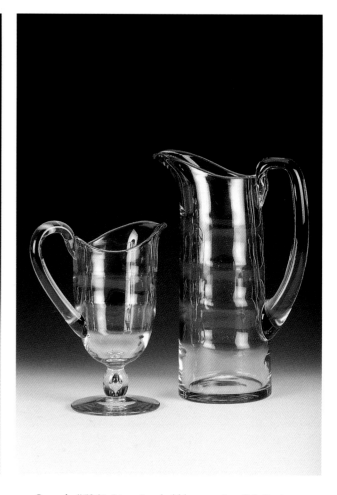

Black #17710 Cordial; Jug, undocumented line number: both with satin finish. **$20-30**; **$75-100**.

Crystal: #15074 Ice Tea; Jug, attributed to Tiffin, undocumented engraving. **$10-15**; **$75-100**.

Crystal: #5961, 24 oz. Jug, bubble stem, Swedish Optic; #5958, 70 oz. Martini Jug, Swedish Optic. **$75-100** each.

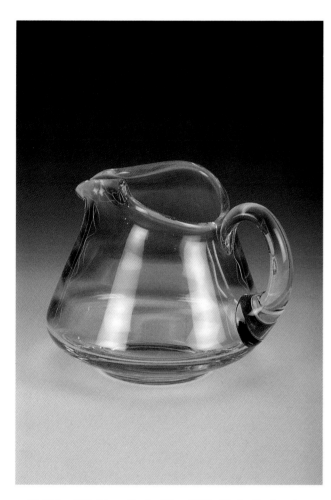

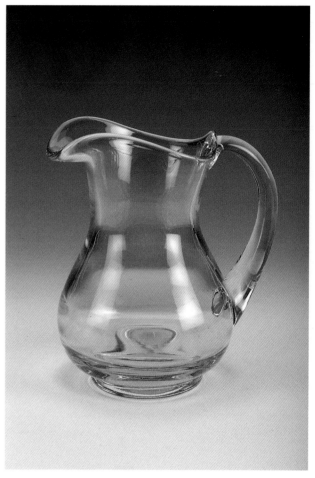

Twilight #12, 24 oz. Cocktail Jug, Tiffin Optic. Produced circa 1953. **$250-300**.

Twilight #4 Ice Lip Jug, Tiffin Optic. **$250-300**.

Twilight #2 Ice Lip Jug, Tiffin Optic, 1955. **$250-300**.

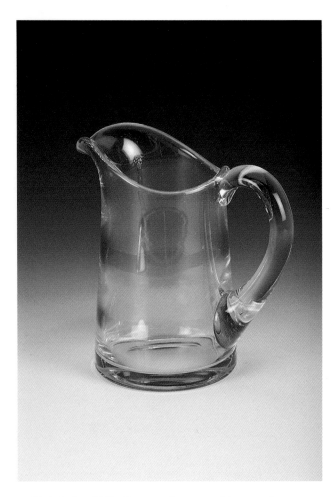

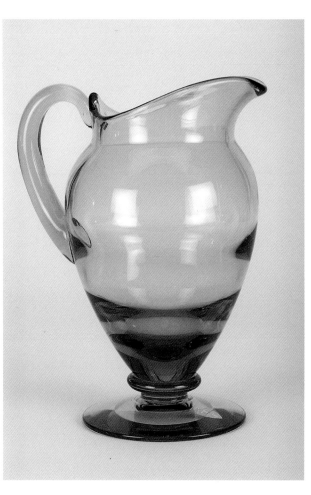

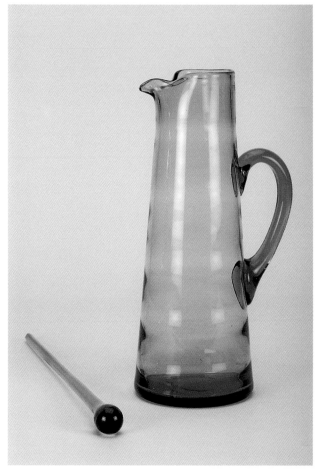

Twilight Jug, Tiffin Optic, undocumented line number. **$175-225**.

Wistaria #6233 Jug, Tiffin Optic. **$500-600**.

Smoke #6349 Martini, with stirrer, Tiffin Optic. **$125-150**.

Copen Blue: #5935 Tankard, #6349, 32 oz. Martini; both Swedish Optic. **$175-200**; **125-150**.

Crystal "Air Trap" Jug with Applied Handle, undocumented line number, c.1976. **$150-200**.

Cocktail Blender, undocumented line number. **$35-45**.

5958 BLOWN MARTINI JUG
Swedish Optic
Capacity—70 oz.

5956 BLOWN COCKTAIL SHAKER
Swedish Optic
Capacity—27 oz.

5956 BLOWN COCKTAIL JUG
Swedish Optic
Capacity—27 oz.

1940 Catalog page.

6233
Jug

6293
Jug

5961
Jug

6294
Ice Lip Jug

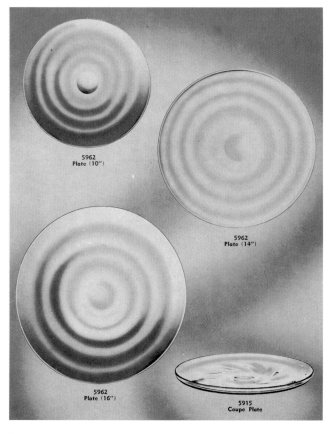

5962
Plate (10″)

5962
Plate (14″)

5962
Plate (16″)

5915
Coupe Plate

1951 Catalog page.

146

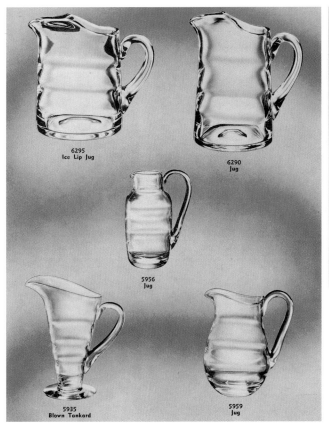

6295
Ice Lip Jug

6290
Jug

5956
Jug

5935
Blown Tankard

5959
Jug

1951 Catalog page.

577 SWEDISH TYPE HANDLED DECANTER
Offhand Globe Stopper   Heavy Base
Capacity—32 oz.

MATCHING WHISKEYS, HEAVY BASE
Capacity—1¼ oz.

No. 5905–33 ... Jug

No. 5905–35 ... Martini Jug

These jugs were introduced in 1947 and discontinued by 1950.

Chapter 13
Accessory Tableware

Included in this chapter are various items that were produced as accessories for the dining room table from 1940 through 1967. Many pressed and blown items were manufactured in Crystal. Some colored ware was also produced.

Top left: Killarney with Crystal trim #6259 Cream and Sugar. The #6259 Cream and Sugar is the same shape as the earlier produced #4 Cream and Sugar. **$125-150** set.

Top right: Desert Red #29 Sugar and Cream, Applied Handles. Also produced in Twilight, Crystal, and Greenbriar, c.1967. **$40-60** set.

Bottom left: Twilight #5411 Small Puritan Cream and Sugar, 1954. **$175-225** set.

Bottom right: Wistaria #5411 Small Puritan Cream and Sugar, produced 1954. **$200-250** set.

Left: Crystal #17578 French Dressing Bottle with cutting. **$45-65**.

Top right: Crystal 6 ¼" h. Cruets, attributed to Tiffin. **$45-65** each.

Bottom right: Detail of cruet engraving.

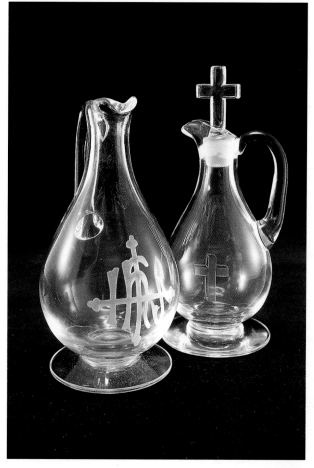

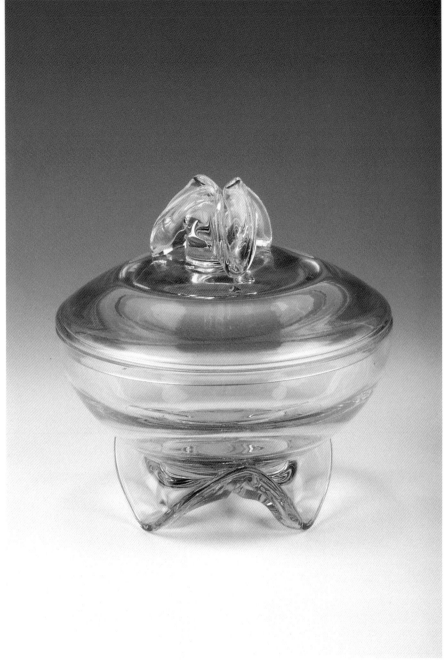

Wistaria with Crystal trim #17423, 11 ½" h. Candy Jar, applied finial, **$275-325**; Wistaria with Crystal trim #17523, 8" h. Covered Candy Box with applied Crown finial, **$275-325**. Both items have Tiffin Optic and are part of the Cellini line.

Twilight #4, 6 ¾" h. Covered Candy Box, with applied Crown finial, Tiffin Optic. **$225-275**.

Plum, Tiffin Rose #6103, 9 ½" h. Candy Box with cover, Diamond Optic, 1961. **$125-150**; **$150-175**.

Cobalt Blue with Crystal trim, Golden Banana #6106, 11 ½" h. Candy Box with Cover, Diamond Optic, 1961. **$200-250**; **$175-200**.

Plum #6102, 4" h. Candle Holders, **$60-75** pair; Golden Banana #6113, 10 ¾" h. Candy Jar with Cover, Diamond Optic, **$175-200**.

Killarney with Crystal trim, #6232, 7" h. Jam Jar. **$100-125.**

Top: Killarney with Crystal trim #6288, 2" footed Salt Dips. The salt dips were known in the 1920-1930 era as the #2 almond cup. **$20-30** each.

Bottom: Killarney with Crystal trim: #6244, 4" h. Cigarette Holder; #17394-7, 3 ¾" h. Footed Cigarette Holder. **$45-65** each.

Wistaria with Crystal trim #17394, 4" h. Candlesticks. These candlesticks were produced to coordinate with the #17394 stemline. **$175-200** pair.

Crystal 7" h. Ice Bucket, metal handle, Tiffin Optic, undocumented line number. **$50-75**.

Chapter 14
Duncan and Miller Patterns by the Tiffin Glass Company

The Duncan and Miller Glass Company of Washington, Pennsylvania, ceased operations on June 24, 1955. The United States Glass Company subsequently purchased a number of Duncan molds and equipment in 1955 and began production of several Duncan patterns in 1956. Operating as the Duncan and Miller Division of the United States Glass Company, production took place at the Glassport, Pennsylvania, and Tiffin, Ohio, factories. A number of Duncan workers followed the molds to these two United States Glass Company factories.

In addition to blown stemware patterns, several popular pressed lines were reproduced, including Canterbury, Early American Sandwich, Georgian, Hobnail, and Tear Drop. Some of these pressed patterns were produced into the 1970s.

Top left: 1956 *Crockery and Glass Journal* advertisement promoting hand made Duncan produced at the Tiffin Glass factory. These were original Tiffin cuttings and stemlines promoted under the Duncan and Miller name.

Bottom left: 1956 *Crockery and Glass Journal* advertisement featuring three original Duncan and Miller Glass Company patterns and stemlines marketed by the United States Glass Company.

Top center: Carefree #D-3. **$15-25**.

Top right: Charmaine Rose #5375. **$20-30**.

Bottom center: Coralbel #D-11. **$15-25**.

Bottom right: Deauville #D-3. **$15-25**.

Top left: Duncan Rose #D-8. **$15-25.**

Top center: Eternally Yours #5331. **$15-25.**

Top right: Fenwick #D-11. **$15-25.**

Bottom left: Garland #5375. **$15-25.**

Bottom center: Juno #5317. **$15-25.**

Above: First Love #5111. The First Love etching was documented in a 1957 United States Glass Company price listing on stemline #5111. This etching was later produced on U.S. Glass (Tiffin) stemline #17453 in 1961. Crystal #5111 Goblet; Cordial. **$20-30; $35-45.**

Right: Detail of First Love etching.

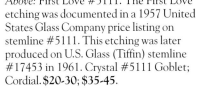

Maytime #5115. **$15-25**.

Remembrance #5115. **$15-25**.

Remembrance #5115: Champagne/Sherbet, Ice Tea, Juice, Cordial. **$15-25**; **$15-25**; **$15-25**; **$25-35**.

Splendor D-15: Goblet and Champagne/Sherbet. **$15-25**; **$10-20**.

Spring Beauty #D-5. **$15-25**.

Willow #D-3: Cocktail, Champagne/Sherbet, Goblet, Ice Tea. **$10-20**; **$10-20**; **$15-25**; **$10-20**.

Canterbury

The Canterbury pattern was originally produced by the Duncan and Miller Glass Company. The United States Glass Company acquired many Duncan and Miller molds and equipment in 1955, then started to produce Canterbury in 1956. Canterbury proved to be a very popular line and was produced through 1980 in many Tiffin Glass colors. Canterbury, which is a pressed pattern, should not be confused with Canterbury II, which is blown ware that was never made by the Duncan and Miller Glass Company. Desert Red #115-5, 13 oz. Footed Ice Tea; Greenbriar #115-13, 5 oz. Juice. **$10-15**; **$5-10**.

Canterbury II

These Canterbury II #17723 stems are shown here to compare with the Canterbury design. Canterbury II was not produced until 1978 and is a blown stem, while all Canterbury is pressed. Twilight #17723: Goblet and Ice Tea. **$15-25** each.

Tear Drop

Tear Drop stemware was produced circa late 1950s from a Duncan and Miller Glass Company mold in Crystal or Smoke. Other tableware items were produced in several Tiffin colors during the 1960s. Crystal #5301-1, 9 oz. Goblets. **$10-15** each.

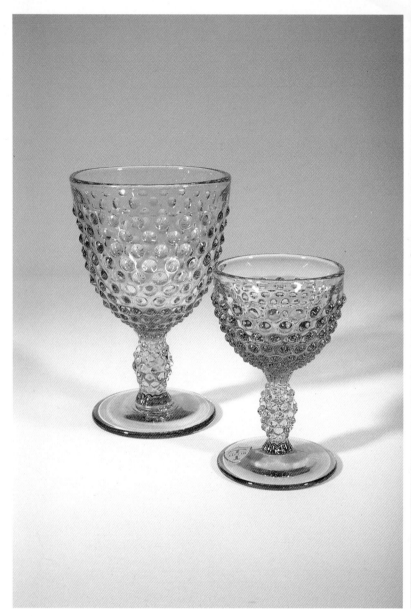

"Handmade by Duncan" paper labels were used by the United States Glass Company from the mid 1950s through the early 1960s. A 1960 interoffice memo stated that all products leaving the factory should have either a Tiffin Glass shield sticker or a Handmade by Duncan label. The Handmade by Duncan label was used on pressed ware, including the Williamsburg line, which was never produced originally by the Duncan and Miller Glass Company.

Hobnail
Produced circa 1963 from a Duncan and Miller Glass Company mold, the Hobnail stemware line was available in the Tiffin colors of Tiffin Rose, Golden Banana, and Plum. Tiffin Rose: #518-1 Goblet; #518-4 Cocktail. **$15-20**; **$10-15**.

Early American Sandwich
When the United States Glass Company purchased a number of Duncan and Miller molds in 1955, the Early American Sandwich Glass pattern #41 was one of several Duncan and Miller lines included. An extensive line in Crystal was produced for Tiffin at their Glassport, Pennsylvania, factory. This pattern was also produced in Milk Glass at Glassport, and marketed as the White Lace #741 line. Two candy jars were manufactured in Plum and Golden Banana at the Tiffin, Ohio, factory, beginning in 1961. Milk Glass: #741-6, 5 oz. Footed Juice; #741-1, 9 oz. Goblets. **$10-15**; **$15-20** each.

Sources

In addition to private archival documents, information for this book was taken from the following sources:

Bickenheuser, Fred. *Tiffin Glassmasters, Book I*. Grove City, Ohio: Glassmasters Publications, 1979.

_____. *Tiffin Glassmasters, Book III*. Grove City, Ohio: Glassmasters Publications, 1985.

China and Glass. Trade magazine. 1940s issues.

China, Glass, and Lamps. Trade magazine. 1940s issues.

Hemminger, Ruth et. al. *Tiffin Modern: Mid-Century Art Glass*. Atglen, Pennsylvania: Schiffer Publishing, Ltd., 1997.

O'Kane, Kelly. *Tiffin Glassmasters, the Modern Years*. St. Paul, Minnesota, 1998.

Page, Bob, and Frederiksen, Dale. *Tiffin is Forever*. Greensboro, North Carolina: Page-Frederiksen Publishing Co., 1994.

Tiffin Glass Company Catalogs and Price Lists: 1967, 1968, 1970-1979.

United States Glass Company Catalogs: 1947, 1955.

Tiffin Glass Collectors Club

The Tiffin Glass Collectors Club is a non-profit corporation with tax exempt status, which was established in 1985 to study the history of Tiffin Glass (known as Factory R) of the United States Glass Company, and the glassware manufactured there.

Membership in the club includes collectors from all over the United States. A club newsletter is published quarterly for members, and features minutes, glass articles, and historical data and other information of interest to collectors.

Activities of the Tiffin Glass Collectors Club include the glass shows held in June and November and fund-raisers to benefit the Tiffin Glass Museum. The Museum is operated by the Tiffin Glass Collectors Club and is located at 25 South Washington Street in downtown Tiffin, Ohio.

For more information on the Club or Museum, inquiries may be directed to Tiffin Glass Collectors Club, P.O. Box 554, Tiffin, Ohio 44883.

Index